The
T'AI CHI
BOXING
Chronicle

The T'AI CHI BOXING Chronicle

By the Original Orthodox Masters

Compiled and Explained by
Kuo Lien-Ying

Translated by
Guttmann

North Atlantic Books
Berkeley, California

The T'ai Chi Boxing Chronicle

Published by
North Atlantic Books
P.O. Box 12327
Berkeley, California 94701–9998

Cover calligraphy by Wing Leong
Cover and book design by Paula Morrison
Typeset by Catherine Campaigne
Printed in the United States of America by Malloy Lithographing

The T'ai Chi Boxing Chronicle is sponsored by The Society for the Study of Native Arts and Sciences, a nonprofit educational corporation whose goals are to develop an educational and crosscultural perspective linking various scientific, social, and artistic fields; to nurture a holistic view of arts, sciences, humanities, and healing; and to publish and distribute literature on the relationship of mind, body, and nature.

Library of Congress Cataloging-in-Publication Data
Kuo, Lien Ying.
    The t'ai chi boxing chronicle / Kuo Lien Ying : translated by Guttmann
        p.   cm.
    Translation of unpublished Chinese manuscript.
    ISBN 1-55643-177-5
        1. T'ai chi ch'uan   I. Title
    GV504.K85   1994
    613.7'148—dc20   93-40412
                                                                    CIP

I   2   3   4   5   6   7   8   9   /   99   98   97   96   95

Preface

Mr. Kuo, my teacher, was a professional in this field and began his studies at the age of twelve. He sought out the finest teachers in China to learn and master Shao Lin, T'ai Chi, Pa Kua, Hsing I, and a multitude of traditional weapons. Each of his serious students received a solid foundation in the physical method and application of these boxing skills. He did not, however, teach the system of **"the true teaching"** for two possible reasons. One is that he did not speak English, although this was not a barrier to those he taught who spoke Chinese; it was a barrier in his transferring the information to students who did not speak his language. The other and more important aspect which would prevent this information being passed down is that the system is a complex set of scientific rules and experiments which require continuous study and application. Comprehension of this and any subject will vary in degree from student to student. Our level of comprehension will be relative to our desire to learn the subject and our ability to understand the information as presented.

Although Mr. Kuo did not orate on this subject as a regular part of the training, a collection or anthology of the classics was assembled and left behind for those who would or could endeavor to pursue such a course of study. The book in your hands is an effort to present this material to the student aspiring to mastery. This collection of articles with commentary was written in a highly complex form of Chinese in most cases and not easily read or translated. The entire system of T'ai Chi boxing is presented in minute detail, and it is not intended for the student to read once and understand. This material must be referenced and cross-referenced many times in order to deduce its meaning and the vital interconnection between chapters. An example of this is the most common word of the T'ai Chi boxing vocabulary, "Ch'i." Most people involved in this art make the assumption that Ch'i is just a general term for some mysterious force which unfortunately no one can define or isolate. If all references to Ch'i in this book are studied and cross-referenced, one can deduce that its meaning is the circulating point of finesse within the body and that Ch'i has a scientific explanation. As a matter of fact, it is stressed many times in the book that all of the concepts of the boxing art are indeed scientific and must be analyzed, not just accepted as generalities.

The original character of the material in Chinese is so complex that I have never met a person who could read the information. Much of the text is written in ancient Chinese which uses fewer characters than the modern form of the language. Occasionally, just one character will be condensed to represent an entire field of knowledge. The later part of the book is written in a more modern form of this language and it is my personal belief that the reason for this type of presentation is to maintain the profound and original content of the system. Mr. Kuo did not create the ancient writings, he compiled them for future generations to inherit. He did however provide explanations because the ancient writings are very difficult if not impossible to understand without a deep background in this art.

The problems of translation were numerous, which is why it took over a decade to arrive at this point in the translation. A good deal of the boxing vocabulary is not in the dictionary but are words restricted only to the boxing art. Many of the words have double meanings. In order to understand the meanings of many words, an etymological approach had to be used which was to learn the root meaning of each character rather than its modern counterpart. This book has never been translated into English before because not only is the language extremely difficult to translate, but it requires a seasoned practitioner to understand the concepts. The translation strictly follows the original text. It is not condensed or reorganized, but there is a small omission of two parts in the beginning what are too arcane for my abilities.

This book is important to Tʼai Chi boxing literature in English and can offer a practitioner the viewpoint of a master who is a scientist and a sage. No aspect of the Yin-Yang theory conflicts with science and logic. Many people in China and America speak of inner strength as an aspect of the spiritual which cannot be defined in concrete terms. Actually inner strength is a physical science which an individual can understand completely as one does mathematics. Mr. Kuo does speak of the spiritual aspect of Tʼai Chi boxing, but only as a result of mastering all of the scientific details of the art.

Foreword

T'ai Chi boxing is often called a secret art, because the system as taught by the ancient masters has been virtually lost. Without proper training in theory and practice, it is not possible to draw out the achievement and master this skill. One can practice the movements for a decade without any comprehension of how they are applied and why. This boxing art is a specific science that is learned step by step to reach the level of what the Chinese call awareness energy. Too many students are left not knowing how to proceed toward full understanding of this skill after the elementary movements have been learned.

This book presents the system of the original orthodox masters who developed the art for survival. T'ai Chi boxing is not a dance. Although the practice movements are soft and slow, the actual use is hard and fast. The purpose of T'ai Chi boxing is on one hand to overcome an enemy, yet on the other it is for self-cultivation. This book explains not only every step that must be taken to achieve the goal of mastery, but also shows the reader how to evaluate his or her progress. In order to progress at this skill, every detail of this knowledge must be questioned persistently. It is simply not adequate to have a vague understanding. Push yourself and do a bitter practice every day without fail. Study the theory of the interplay of Yin and Yang. Reach the level of knowing and not guessing.

Acknowledgments

Professor Kuo Lien Ying—My teacher whose teaching system gave students a solid foundation. This book is a translation and interpretation of the text he left behind in order to preserve a perfected boxing system handed down by the ancients.

Mr. Bing Leong—An example of endurance and the qualities that a sincere student should possess.

Mr. Kimo Lepree—His unending devotion to the art and skill of T'ai Chi boxing is an inspiration.

Mr. Ch'en Bing Ch'uan—For his contributions in translation and his sincere enthusiasm for an art which is virtually lost today.

Mr. Steve Lockwood—My student who appeared in the dark of every morning to strive for perfection.

Mr. Wing Leong (Chinese Art Studio)—For providing the artwork of the title Chinese characters.

And to all of the students who have made T'ai Chi boxing a lifestyle and reap its rich harvest.

Table of Contents

The
T'AI CHI
BOXING
Chronicle

The Overview

The Yin-Yang Reversal Theory

Yang is Heaven, sky, sun, and fire imparting a force to the body. Then Yin meets Yang. Yin is the rolling into one, the earth, moon, and water. It is a holding force and the philosophy that combines our bones, flesh, and heart. It is the place where science and philosophy walk hand in hand. Take a deep breath and be still to understand the reversing of Yin and Yang.

Fire and Water: Think carefully for a long time and it will be understood. Fire rises and water flows down. water can put the fire out when placed on top. This is the reversing. It is a natural law and never changes. However, when the water flows down and you place a pot under it to stop it from reaching its extreme limit, and you place fire under the pot and stop it from reaching its extreme limit, the result is the boiling of water. This is called the Yin-Yang reversal theory that allows one to make use of the natural laws. The T'ai Chi boxing system is based on this reversal theory, which is used in every aspect of the skill. This is the relationship of fire and water. If the fire only rises up and the water only flows down, there will be two separate bodies called fire and water not working together.

Two are two; combine them to become one. One can be two, two can be one, called the three: sky, earth, and the people. Once the Yin-Yang reversal philosophy is understood, then one will realize that the two cannot be separated. Sky above and earth below and the people in between. If one studies the sky and the earth, understands the sun and moon, knows all of the elements, the seasons, the grass and woods, the good and evil, the good and bad luck of one's life, then Yin and Yang will be understood as the larger body and people as the smaller body. One's body and soul are combined to evaluate matters. When we understand the concept of Yin and Yang we can express the Tao. We can understand heaven and earth and can reason out what motivates people, and why some people seem to have bad luck and some good. Then we can ascend to our most intelligent level. If one does not lose one's thoughts one can make use of the goodness in oneself. We can develop it because the boundary of growth is endless! The body can create a small universe of its own. One's mind is the earth, one's life is the person, and one's soul is the energy. If one cannot understand, how can one be equal to heaven and earth? The outcome of life is not entirely up to fate. There is work of our own for the making, the future that is to come.

The T'ai Chi Body

T'ai Chi means the center. The two eyes are the sun and moon, the two elements of Yin and Yang. The head is the sky and the feet are the earth; the person within the person is the inner self. Combined they are the three in one. The four limbs are the four seasons. Kidney is water, heart is fire, liver is wood, lungs are metal, and the diaphragm is earth. These are Yin. Bladder is water, small intestine is fire, pancreas is wood, large intestine is metal, and stomach is earth. These are Yang.

Left ear is metal, right ear is wood. Energy comes from the heart, and the eyes are the "stems" of thoughts collected from the brain, nourished by the kidney, and breathed through the lungs.

Water is salty, wood is sour, earth is spicy, fire is bitter, and metal is sweet. Applied to one's voice wood is bright, fire is rough or gutteral, metal is soft, earth is loud, and water is smooth.

The following represent the eight trigrams called the Pa Kua:

K'an	north	water	kidney
Chen	east	wood	liver
Tui	west	metal	lung
Ch'ien	northwest	metal to water	large intestine
K'un	southwest	earth	spleen
Hsun	southeast	water to earth	gallbladder
Ken	northeast	earth to water	stomach
Li	south	fire	heart

The Pa Kua are numbered as follows:

1. K'an
2. K'un
3. Chen
4. Hsun
5. The center of T'ai Chi
6. Ch'ien
7. Tui
8. Ken
9. Li

Numbers two and four are the shoulders, and six and eight are the feet. Number one is under nine. Left is three, and right is seven.

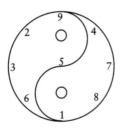

The Pa Kua Diagram

T'ai Chi Balance

The body is like a scale. It is an ancient dictum that the top of the head should be held as though suspended from above. The hands are the plates which balance the right and left. The waist must be level like the base of a tree with its roots above the ground. Stand like a scale so that the light and heavy or rising and falling can be measured to the smallest degree. Any leaning is a defect. The top of the head is suspended with the waist as the root. There must be a straight line between the top of the head, the chest, and the middle of the waist. This is what allows one to turn and revolve. The body measures like a scale and revolves. The intention commands the Ch'i like a flag, naturally. Make the body light and sharp so it can become the perfect body. This way the coming and going or entering and retreating will not be early or late. Balance will be fully analyzed in upcoming chapters. Balance must be learned and it is the first step to progress.

T'ai Chi Stillness and Action

Stillness is the foundation and action is the use. Action is the achievement of stillness. This is what is called the spirit of vitality. Stillness is the foundation of the mind and body's action. This blending of stillness and action is a Taoist alchemy and is the root of true physical education. The storing up and releasing is the basis of striking. Stillness without action is of no use, and action without the companion of stillness has no foundation. Don't think that the action part of physical education alone is the achievement. All things follow this principle. If you are only brave, it won't defeat an enemy. If you only are still and calm, likewise you will lose. So, to use this system against men you must implement stillness and action together like the Yin and Yang.

Awareness Energy

To become skilled, four fundamental defects must be corrected. They are:

1. Muscle against muscle
2. Stiffness
3. Getting rid of the opponent
4. Resisting

Four other defects must be corrected which are related to the first four:

1. Being intermittent
2. Receiving a person's energy straight instead of curved
3. Leaning forward
4. Leaning backward

When these defects are corrected, the opponent's motion, direction, and speed can be intuited instantly. This energy or skill is learned through the practice of push hands. Learn to listen to the gradual, quick, hard, and soft. This ability is not a result of seeing and hearing. The sureness of an exact answer is from feeling. Attaining this stage of skill is difficult. This method is explained below clearly and in detail. Strive to attain this energy and in the future there will be little concern about the body, as the body will take care of itself.

Enlightenment Through Action

Reason is the supreme power of the two Ch'is, Yin and Yang. This is the Chinese power principle which equals heaven and earth, with the Tao as the center. The concept of Yin and Yang is the Taoist attainment. It's the interplay of the two, one Yin and one Yang. This is the Tao which has no name. Before heaven and earth were born there was Wu Chi or nothingness, which has no name. After the world came into existence it was named Yu Chi and it has a name.

Before heaven and earth there was a reason, and when the world was born came the mother. The mother was born in heaven's embryo and gave birth to all things. The Tao was its center. Heaven and earth are the great father and mother. The earth father and mother are called the small father and mother. The Ch'i of before and after creation descended from the heavens, and the earthly parents then came as the human body, the original natural gift of the great father and mother. From the small father and mother come the blood, form, and skeleton.

To unite the before-creation and after-creation brings us personal destiny. From this we get the successful man and woman who equals heaven and earth from the three sources. Follow your natural disposition and you won't miss the target. If you intend to seek out the place, come to the source, open the gate, and achieve good results. How do we learn this intangible thing? Wise and foolish, capable or not, all can enter Tao. The Tao must be cultivated, so come to the source to know it. The Gods can't repair it if you miss. Anyone can become an emperor if they cultivate themselves. How can one cultivate instinct, inborn ability, vision, and hearing? With the proper attitude and good faith, the feet stomp the five steps called Wu Hsing and the hands dance the eight gates called the Pa Kua. Feet and hands are the four seasons. They use special means to get to the source. The eyes see the three combinations. Ear, eye, hand, and foot divided are two, combined are one, and collectively are T'ai Chi. The outside is held together by the inside. So it's said, be content with one's lot. Heaven's way, man's way; one warning and that is all.

Chapter One

The Creation of the
T'ai Chi Boxing Principles

What is T'ai Chi Wu Tang Boxing? T'ai Chi is a specialized form of boxing art. Its history is ancient. It is written in the fifteen chapters of the Sung family chronicles that the oldest known records stem from the time of the T'ang dynasty, and that the information was recorded by Hsu Hsuan P'ing , whose nickname was Yu Kuan Tze. These records also date from the time period of Ch'ang Sung Hsi, when the lives of seven famous men and their skills were recorded. Their names were:

> Sung Yuan Ch'iao
> Yin Li Liang
> Yu Tai Yeh
> Mo Ku Sheng
> Ch'ang Tsui Shan
> Yu Lien Chou
> Ch'ang Sung Hsi

Some of these seven men learned from master Ch'ang San Feng, the acknowledged founder of the T'ai Chi boxing system, and some learned from master Li. Master Ch'ang and Master Li arrived together at Wu Tang mountain and together founded what became the Wu Tang school of boxing art.

This same history is also revealed in the chronicles of Ch'en Ch'ang Hsing, which were begun by Wang Tsung Yueh, who passed down the original words of Ch'ang San Feng. These records prove that the earliest mention of T'ai Chi boxing is from the time of the T'ang dynasty, 618–907 A.D. There is evidence that Master Ch'ang San Feng actually learned the system as passed down from the time of Hsu Hsuan P'ing. There is no record of how or why the Ch'en family received the Wang chronicles. The introduction says it was during the last part of the Ming dynasty; however, it is not entirely clear. These chronicles are comprised of forty-three chapters regarding boxing theory and contain the essentials of T'ai Chi boxing. All of the terminology is explained, but in a different way than is currently taught in T'ai Chi boxing.

In this book we will examine the Ch'en family treasure, the chronicles that were hidden for nine generations until the time of Ch'en Wang T'ing, near the end of the Ming dynasty or in the beginning of the Ch'ing dynasty. Ch'en Wang T'ing was a skilled boxer and represented the tradition of the Ch'en family. At this point a man named Chiang P'u modified the Ch'en family form. Then the style was divided into the old set and the new set as modified by Chiang P'u. This division is very evident today. Naturally the old set is the Ch'en family's original set. It was recorded that Chiang P'u never attained the skill of Ch'en Wang T'ing, so the reason for altering the already-polished boxing art is unknown.

The original set was in accordance with the ideas of the Pa Kua and Wu Hsing, and it was arranged into thirteen sections called the thirteen forces. The new set uses many hand movements but is often contrary to the principles of the boxing art. You can accept or refuse the new method or the Wu Tang method but don't dare to reach a conclusion too quickly. It is not easy to distinguish whether the movements are the real moving energy of T'ai Chi boxing. It seems that only the Wu Tang system was published for future generations. In the chronicles of the honorable Ch'en family, all of the key points are made clear and the text is very long. There is not one chapter which does not mention Ch'en Ch'ang Hsing's Wang chronicles.

We really don't know which dynasty Wang Tsung Yu was born in. Some say the Ming, some say the Ch'ing, but hand-written documents say both so there is no way of knowing.

Study and research the essentials of Wu Tang boxing. Look at the root of this fantastic moving energy. The rules and principles are all for practical use. All of the books—Sung, Wang, Ch'en, Yang, Li, and Huang—contain priceless information. Try to grasp the principles and attain the function of their profound meaning. Then, like following the footprints of history, enter the gate of the method. How to make use of the spirit of vitality is pointed out. Combined, these books are without defect. Think and meditate on these six books which record the sets and their structure. Don't decide too quickly; be absolutely sure. Are the teachings the same or not? The old set and the newer set are different but both will be passed down for a thousand years!

If you deviate from the main road, you won't get the full benefit of T'ai Chi boxing's Wu Tang school. There is a total of one hundred chapters written by the six families above. The first chapter outlines T'ai Chi boxing, and the second chapter is the Wang chronicle, called "Kung Hsin Chieh." These two chapters guide one in evaluating progress. They completely explain the uses of the spirit of vitality which is learned through push hands. You cannot disregard the rules. What is left behind from the oldest time until now is a boxing art to assimilate. Understanding these two chapters creates an indomitable person. Research and study these two chapters, which are the creation of the principles. There it says: There are many misleading ways of teaching the art and skill of boxing. Although differing from one another, they all share a common principle which is that the strong beat the weak and the slow yield to the fast. These are theories not based on true knowledge and philosophical research. It is obvious that strength alone does not explain a thousand pounds toppled with a trigger force of four ounces. When an old man defends himself against a number of young people, something more than mere strength and speed is involved.

This kind of circumstance is why the T'ai Chi boxing principles were created. One studies theory in order to overcome brute force. The skill of the weak beating the strong must be forged in method. First there are restrictions in movement, afterwards the principles are the only restrictions. The boxing chronicles include everything in their sphere. Do not disregard this science. Make use of the two principles as follows:

The Weak Beats the Strong

According to the T'ai Chi boxing principles and theories, the body must move like a screw or spiral. Its function is like that of a lever. Picture a train with many cars derailing. When one uses a screwing or spiral form, the lever revolves the top of the thousand pounds and many cars are thrown off the tracks. This is the light forcing the heavy. Compare the boxing chronicle's rule: Moving energy must be like reeling in silk. The bent takes over the straight, and the soft conquers the hard—that is the method.

The Slow Beats the Fast

According to the T'ai Chi theory, you must reach the inside of the circle to be effective by means of centrifugal force. Picture a wheel three feet in diameter and an axle of one foot. If the axle turns forty-five degrees, the result is a movement of 1.177 feet on the outer rim of the wheel. But on the axle itself the result is 3.92 inches, a ratio of three to one. So, use the center point instead of the outside.

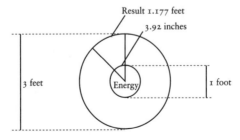

In other words, it takes three seconds on the outside to move a foot and only one second on the axle. This is how the Ch'i is like a wheel and the waist is like an axle. You are the last one to action, but the first to the point. This is the essential of the method.

When these two principles are understood, one will see that the axle drags the opponent by revolving. To be effective, friction or rubbing must occur. This pulling energy is called Lu ching. If this screwing action cannot be used, then the opponent cannot be turned. In the event the two opponents mutually resist each other, then the spiral is impeded and the opponent cannot be turned. If one intends to correct this undesirable situation, one must possess the characteristics of the inside being hard and the outside being soft, and the body must abound with flexibility. The center point of the body can be said to resemble a steel wire and the outside a rubber band; then friction can be born.

Peng ching, is very important. In the event one encounters hard and solid strength, one must especially bore in and revolve. Heaviness must be added to Peng ching in order to succeed. Chi ching comes into play and reverses the direction of Peng. Most people have their root equally under both feet. When the opponent is turned by effecting a tugging motion on his root, bore in and revolve. The tugging motion naturally slants downward in order to follow. Make the smallest response happen and then the opponent will not slip away and his movements will become confused. Then An ching follows.

These four forces (Peng, Lu, Chi, and An) allow one to spiral from the axle and revolve. The proof of the working of these four forces comes when one can oppose the other's body without hindrance. These four forces are used in ordinary movements, not just for special movements. When meeting an opponent, be determined not to move your body. Be neither coming nor going, but afterwards put into operation the sticking connection. To misuse this pulling action is a defect.

The opponent is prevented from getting away through the use of Tsai ching, which is a kind of grabbing and sticking action. It is like plucking or picking fruit from a tree. From the use of Tsai, grabbing and bone-locking techniques are born. Completely rely on the opponent's movements, then reverse and change his body from whatever movement he has made. In other words, this is a way of upsetting the opponent's center of gravity. One must especially string together all of the movements, one after another. Then you meet the opponent in between and get the result of the power. You stick and connect.

How do you strike the opponent? If the sticking is not accurate, if it is too light or too heavy, this is undesirable. The touch must be just right to get this sticking connection. If it is not exact, an adjustment is necessary. K'ung, Chieh, Tso, and Jou will be implemented to stick properly.

> **K'ung** (empty)   drains the opponent's energy
> **Chieh** (tie up) adds to the opponent's energy
> **Tso**   (break)   drains energy and causes his posture
>   to deteriorate
> **Jou**   (rub)   is empty and divides strength

These four forces are called the adjustment machine. When you use this, proper sticking will result. Furthermore, the four adjustments are concealed in rolling and releasing. Rolling is the large circle changing to the small circle. Releasing is the small circle changing to the large circle. Remember the diagram. Roll and release are the foundation of pulling and dragging. They are contained in the sticking connection.

The body weight must sink to one side. It is a kind of power. It is the power of empty and solid. This sinking to one side is the beginning of revolving. You roll up and release, then from the pulling everything comes to the exterior from this energy. If the rolling and releasing reach the zenith point, then it becomes collecting and striking. Collecting is like drawing a bow, and the strength of flexibility is added. Collecting will change the direction of an impact.

When striking, the direction and method are different. Then

Lieh, Chou, and K'ao come into play. The waist and the spine move to let the arrow go. The strike must be issued at the opponent's center of gravity in order to be effective. This is using centripetal force. The main principle is that when trying to use this centripetal force, the body must be centered to get the power. If the body's balance is correct, then you can borrow the energy of another. Heavy and light energy can be borrowed. Get the feeling of the path of "adhere and evade," through which one comes to understand awareness energy. The principle of T'ai Chi boxing is scientific judgment and analysis. The six main points are as follows:

1. **Centrifugal Force** — T'ai Chi boxing's vital element of motion.

2. **Returning the Line** — T'ai Chi boxing's path of motion.

3. **Friction and Flexibility** — T'ai Chi boxing's offense and defense, the preparation of active strength.

4. **Deviation of the Center of Gravity** — Starting the movement of T'ai Chi.

5. **Rolling, Collecting, Releasing, and Striking** — T'ai Chi boxing's strategy and military tools.

6. **Centripetal Force** — T'ai Chi boxing's striking power.

These principles are from the chapter "Kung Hsin Chieh," which presents all of these points in detail. This will aid in the study of boxing and in understanding the principles. Think about learning boxing today. It is very confusing. You may ask someone and they may tell you that they know, but they don't. They go in a leader and leave a servant. So, it's not easy to make a judgment without a sound foundation. You have to examine all of the details and complexities.

In China much of the boxing is modern and fashionable, but the movements are often contradictory to the principles of the T'ai

Chi boxing art. Many people practice the sets and don't know what they are practicing. Originally the skill of boxing was deep and profound. The original skill can be used against men. One must question and question persistently to gain its full use. From the orthodox masters the answers can be found; otherwise, how can one determine if what you are practicing belongs to the boxing art or not?

Naturally it is not easy to draw a conclusion as to whether or not weakness can beat strength, or if the slow can beat the fast. One must question these circumstances. Don't dare to criticize whether a set is good or bad. In ancient times there were many schools. Today we have the same problem and it is not surprising. If one intends to enter the gate of learning without a standard, how will one proceed? There are so many teachers, how will you know which one can pass on the real art? This boxing is ancient knowledge and must be forged. We are lucky that many boxing chronicles were left behind as a guide for practice.

In this text is the chapter "Kung Hsin Chieh." Read it thoroughly and etch it into your brain. This is a formula, an example which will enable you to proceed. In "Kung Hsin Chieh" the rules are all examined and reviewed. These are instructions which measure your progress. Make great effort to seek out this skill. Again, practice push hands in order to use T'ai Chi boxing. This way one won't make the mistake of straying from the main path. Use the two principles above as the standard. Learn the achievement of the hard and soft. Then you will not be attacked and destroyed. Study and ask yourself, what is the real T'ai Chi boxing? You can use Huang Pai's "four key points" or Wang Tsung Yueh's "Kung Hsin Chieh" to get the answers. These are the orthodox teachings handed down from the masters. This way you won't be undecided. In every aspect, research and study!

Chapter Two

The Three Steps of T'ai Chi Boxing

The meaning of the chapter "Kung Hsin Chieh" is profound. The language of the text is complex, but everything is discussed. Practice according to this chapter. One must investigate and study the set and the principles in order to transmit the theory into practice.

Step One: Investigate the Body, the Form, the Waist, the Top of the Head, the Spine, and the Steps

1. The body

Boxing chronicles say that the body must be centered and comfortable. It must be able to handle impact from any direction. The center of the waist and the top of the head must be in a straight line as though a line were drawn between them. To be centered is paramount. When the body is centered it can handle impact from any direction! If one leans forward, the back cannot respond. If the body slants to the left or right, one side of the body will not be able to respond. If the body is centered it stands on safe ground.

Be like a wheel, then the body can revolve in any direction. Be centered and don't move like a great flag. This is T'ai Chi boxing's art of maneuvering the body in self-defense. If the body is centered, the waist energy will be stable. You are relaxed, not impeded. This is having lively strength. The body can support impact from any direction. Then all sides of the body have Peng ching, or resilience. It is undesirable to lean or incline the body in any direction because then the body has some area without Peng ching. This is a shortcoming and means that "the axle is bent" and thus the body cannot revolve. When practicing the set, pay attention; it is easy to fall back into bad habits.

Examples:

1. In Brush knee and twist step, there should be no leaning forward.
2. In Step up apparent close up, there should be no leaning backwards.
3. In Part the wild horse's mane, there should be no slanting or inclining.
4. In Single whip step down, there should be no slanting or leaning.

2. The form

Boxing chronicles say that the practitioner's form should be like a hawk seizing a rabbit, and the spirit is like a cat catching a mouse. In order to arouse the Ch'i, the body must be able to revolve without impediment. The form comes from the inside. When T'ai Chi boxing is practiced the spirit is lively and the spirit of vitality is aroused. Practice the Ch'i returning to Spirit. When the force of the Ch'i is transferred, the spirit of vitality is concentrated, and when the wheel is pulled it can revolve unhindered. If the spirit of vitality cannot be aroused, then the form appears dull. The eyes should be fixed and the body moves around smooth and light in any direction. Like the hawk pouncing on the rabbit. If the spirit is not lively and can't be aroused, the energy can't revolve. How can you expect to revolve like a wheel if the wheel is blocked?

Questions:

1. Can you arouse the spirit of vitality?

2. Is the spirit lively and concentrated, like a cat catching a mouse?

3. The waist

Boxing chronicles say that the waist is like an axle, and the spine is the great streamer-flag pole. The Ch'i is threaded to the top of the head, which gives strength of movement to the body. Stand upright on the body's base and take heed of the waist and spine. Inside, the abdomen is loose and the Ch'i can jump out. The waist is in charge; it is the basis of moving energy. The centrifugal force revolving on the axle is the foundation of the slow overcoming the fast. If the waist is not centered or if the axle is bent, the body cannot revolve. When you practice the set, examine the revolving motion. Does it start from the waist? Is it loose? Do you stand firm like a mountain? These observations help to investigate the T'ai Chi boxing waist.

Questions:

1. In Carry tiger to mountain, does the waist twist?
2. In Chop opponent with fist, does the waist collect energy?
3. In Fair lady works at shuttles, do the top of the head and waist work together?
4. In Cross wave of water lily, does the power of the kick come from the waist?

In the above situations, the waist should be striking from the center of gravity. This is called T'ai Chi's waist.

4. The top of the head

Boxing theory says that the head is upheld with the intangible spirit. The Ch'i sinks to the Tan T'ien, which is the body's center of gravity, located three inches below the navel. When the spirit of vitality is aroused you won't have to worry about being late or early. So it is said, the head is "suspended from above." Hold the body in a central position. Practice what you have learned regarding the idea of lively power like the wheel. The Ch'i is threaded to the top, and the hands, light and empty, conform to the opponent. In summary, the top energy must be empty and light, and the spirit of vitality is aroused. Then the body is natural. If the top does not rise lightly, then the top has no Peng ching. If the body leans backward or forward or to the side, then the body is not balanced. The posture of the head must be studied while the movements twist and change.

Questions:

1. In Slow palm slanting, flying, is the top of the head slanted?
2. In Wave hands like clouds, does the top of the head wobble or sway?
3. In Chop opponent with fist, does the top of the head lean forward?
4. In Repulse the monkey, is the top of the head off-center?

If the above defects are not present in the set, then you can say that this is T'ai Chi boxing's top of the head.

5. The spine

Boxing classics say that when pushing or pulling, the strength comes from the spine. The Ch'i sticks to the back. The source of the power is in the spine and waist. When moving this way, the waist is the axle and the hands are the wheel. If the Ch'i does not stick to the back, the chest will protrude and the shoulders will rise. Then you have hand movements which are not the body's movements. If the Ch'i sticks to the back, the shoulders will sink and the chest will be normal. When practicing the set, study the in and out or coming and going of the pulling motion. Feel whether the back has any fluctuations. Striking movements cannot be issued from the back unless the shoulders are sunk.

Questions:

> 1. In Part the wild horse's mane, does the Ch'i stick to the back?
> 2. In Deflect, parry, and punch, does the strike come from the back?
> 3. In Grasp the bird's tail, when the hands sink back, does this sinking come from the spine?
> 4. In Fan through the arm, does the arm get its strength from the back?

If you comply with the above, you will have T'ai Chi boxing's spine.

6. The steps

Boxing classics say step like a cat. They also say that the steps follow the revolving body. The feet should not be pigeon-toed or bow-legged. When you step like a cat, the heel steps to the front light and empty and upon arrival it arrives it becomes solid. When the body turns, the steps follow. Never step and then turn the body, or the form will have defects. The steps will not fit, and this defect will influence the whole body and cause confusion of the steps. If you are pigeon-toed, your step is easily broken. If you are bow-legged, then you can't keep your balance.

Pay attention to the hips. The hips should be threaded between the feet and the top of the head. If the body is centered it is easy to walk like a cat and obtain a good position. In turning naturally, first the body turns and then the steps move in accordance with the body. However, when you enter or retreat, first you step and then the body follows. Although the body does not twist when entering or retreating, the waist energy is still usable. The body can twist if required. If you don't walk like a cat catching a mouse— first empty and then solid—you will not remain in balance. It's not easy for the Ch'i to move without Peng ching. When you practice the set use your utmost effort and pay attention to the steps because they are the body's root. Investigate all of the steps. Are they empty to solid? In order to obtain a good position, the steps must be skillful.

Questions:

1. In Single whip, after the stride, is the head centered with the groin?
2. In Brush knee and twist step, is the heel empty and afterwards solid?
3. In Deflect, parry, and punch, is there the defect of the body following the steps?
4. In Carry tiger to mountain, is there the defect of the stride being broken?

Step Two: Study Moving, Receiving, Collecting and Striking Energy

1. Moving energy

The boxing chronicles say that moving energy is like drawing silk. They also say that moving energy is like tempering steel a hundred times. Let's analyze these two statements.

Investigate these two characters. In all boxing movements you draw silk, and it is the spiral form which causes outward and inward lines. All movements must utilize these motions. In the outward drawing of silk, the fingers draw from the heel. In the inward drawing of silk, the heel draws the fingers back. This causes an intersecting line. Left foot, right hand; right foot, left hand. The outward drawing of silk is also called opening and the inward drawing of silk is called closing. Opening and closing energy are separate and clearly divided in every T'ai Chi boxing movement. The profound meaning of T'ai Chi boxing is that although the moving energy is in and out, the inner energy is really round.

Moving energy is like tempering steel one hundred times. Moving energy is the degree of hard and soft. When steel is tempered it becomes extremely pliable. Consider the essentials of hardness. Because of softness, more hardness can be added. The hardness is forged to a greater degree on the inside, and the outside is to a greater degree soft. This is called T'ai Chi's extreme softness and afterwards extreme hardness. So, T'ai Chi boxing's softness is not at all like the softness of cotton. It is much different. The outside is soft but the inside is hard. This inner hardness is called Ch'i Kung and it creates Peng ching. The body is both soft and hard. These two modes are essential.

Now you are ready for T'ai Chi boxing's theorem. This twisting movement of the wheel must be like steel. It is not easy for the wheel to be broken when it is moving swiftly. The wheel won't break because it is solid. This is how the slow overcomes the fast. The connection is the revolving of the "drawing of silk" motion and then returning it. The light can overcome the heavy.

When you practice the set, study all of the movements. Do they follow the spiral going out and in? You must observe this spiral fully; it is not enough to go half-way. This line of moving energy must be studied. In particular you must absorb the concept of the inside being hard and the outside being soft, and the degree of hard and soft. Again, study softness. Is the Peng ching soft? The softness of cotton, for example, is not resilient which means that it has no Peng ching. One must know how to read Peng ching, to determine whether or not there is enough. If all of the movements have the right degree of Peng ching and the spiral form is followed in and out, then you have the idea of the outside being soft and the inside being hard. Then you can say it is T'ai Chi's real moving energy.

Examples:

1. In Part the wild horse's mane, when the drawing of silk is out and in are there any breaks?
2. In Wave hands like clouds (double outward drawing of silk), are there any breaks when you move to the left or right?

3. In Grasp the bird's tail (outward and inward drawing of silk), are there any breaks when you expand or contract?

4. In Brush knee and twist step, when you go side to side, are there any breaks?

5. Are all of the movements relaxed? This energy does not permit exertion in its use.

6. Are all movements focused and do they match your intention? Is there any wasted movement?

7. Do all revolving movements contain Peng ching? Are there any inactive or stiff movements?

The above examples contain the twelve elements of drawing of silk which will be discussed at great length in this text. This is the method of the outside being soft and the inside hard. Gain the benefit from this drawing of silk and your movements will have no breaks. How the light overcomes the heavy will be understood when the purpose of moving energy is grasped. If the body is empty inside but without Peng ching it is called a wheel of cotton and is of no use. This is not the purpose of T'ai Chi boxing's moving energy. When the body is soft but does not contain Peng ching, the inside is not solid and hard. Then there is no movement of drawing of silk on the inside, and this is not T'ai Chi boxing's moving energy.

2. Receiving energy

Boxing theory says that folding must be continuously incorporated in the movements. When you intend to turn upward, you first begin from below. If you want to go to the front, you must begin from the rear. Left and right also follow this principle. In other words, when a drawing of silk comes to an end in any direction, folding must be used to make it complete. If folding is not used with moving energy, the power is hard and stiff. T'ai Chi boxing flows smoothly with no breaks, like the Yangtze river. Rely on folding and string the movements together so that you are always connected to the opponent. When folding is used, you can always return again and remain connected. To receive is to release, to release is to receive. There is receiving energy in every movement. If you want to receive upward then you must fold from below. If you intend to go to the left, you must first fold from the right. This reasoning applies to all directions and then Peng ching is forever unbroken.

Study all of the movements of the set. They must be continuous. It is of the utmost importance to pay attention to receiving. Then you will be able to enter and receive the opponent's energy at the same time. This is how to get T'ai Chi boxing's power.

Examples of folding:

1. When raising the hand in White stork cools its wings, fold from beneath and then go up.
2. In White stork cools its wings, when you brush the knee, your intention is to go down so the folding is from the top.
3. In Brush knee and twist step, you intend to go back so fold from the front.
4. When receiving in Carry tiger hand, you intend to go right so fold from the left.
5. When you receive in Brush knee and twist step, you intend to go forward but must first fold from behind.
6. In Carry tiger to mountain, you intend to go to the left so first fold from the right.

The above examples refer to folding. When receiving energy you are connected and threaded without end. T'ai Chi boxing's moving energy is continuous and complete. In every move the start must be slow and the finish is fast. Peng ching is increased. A great degree of Ch'i is used. When coming together with an opponent, a degree of slowness exists but the actual use of folding is fast.

While practicing the set, you can alternate between slow and fast without confusion of movement. This is called clarity. When you move, do not separate folding and drawing of silk; otherwise the spirit will be dulled and the wheel will not get the power from the combination of long distance and slowness. When the opponent's movement is excited and quick, then respond quickly. If the movement is gradual, then gradually follow!

3. Collecting energy

The boxing chronicles say that collecting energy is like the drawing of a bow. Collecting energy has a surplus. There must be flexibility because without it you cannot measure or estimate the bow. The hands and feet must have Peng ching, and the entire body must be threaded together and continuous. Inside, the Ch'i is stored. If all these factors are present, then the bow measurement will work. If any part of the body is not threaded together or does not have Peng ching, then when you draw the bow it will break at the joint. This cannot be called a flexible bow. The line or circuit of collecting energy incorporates rolling energy. The energy is inside and is a part of drawing of silk. On a curved line the body rolls and collects energy. It is the back which makes the bow and leads the collecting energy. If it is broken you don't have collecting energy. Not only can you not increase flexibility, you cannot return the flexibility as a strike.

When you practice the set, study every single movement. Does it have Peng ching? Does it contain collecting energy inside? If you have this then you have the achievement of collecting. Study and investigate whether every move is consistently threaded together. If you have satisfied these requirements, then you can draw the bow. Rolling and collecting energy greatly increase flexibility; it is called "opening the bow ready to fire."

Questions:

> 1. In receiving and returning with a strike (inward drawing of silk), if there is activity on the right side, does the left side collect?

2. In Deflect downward, parry, and punch, does the energy suddenly collect and is it outward drawing of silk?

3. In Strike the tiger force, does the energy collect gradually and is it outward drawing of silk? Is the collecting curved?

4. In High pat on horse, the energy is divided collecting. Inside there is outward and inward drawing of silk. Is there front and back collecting energy?

5. In Apparent close up, is it connecting and collecting energy?

If you conform to the above, then you can measure your degree of flexibility. You can estimate the bow's strength or weakness; you can draw the bow to a greater or lesser degree. If there is no Peng ching, then it is not easy to be threaded together. So, when you practice the set, the collecting energy's power should be concealed; otherwise it will not embody the idea of martial arts skill. Furthermore, in order to express refinement you must grasp the idea of rolling. If the rolling is not complete, it is called empty and hollow. It cannot be called collecting energy's "skeleton."

4. Striking energy

The boxing chronicles say that striking energy is like releasing an arrow because the strength is shot from the spine. Striking energy and collecting energy are related to each other like the Yin and Yang. First comes the collecting and then the striking. Striking is born from collecting. The striking gains force from the foundation of collecting. When the bow's strength or weakness is known, the energy is collected in a curved way. The rolling energy lets you have a surplus.

When you strike, it must be rooted in the principle of releasing. Then there will be more than enough of T'ai Chi boxing's striking energy. In other types of boxing the principle of striking is different. To seek the straight from the curved is the boxing chronicle's rule. Don't straighten out the hand one hundred percent when you seek the straight from the curved. When the hand is not completely extended, the striking energy may be discontinued but the Peng ching is still there. Receiving energy can be used to continue extensions of the strike without a break. If the striking energy has no break, then it can't continue outward, and this can't be called striking. But Peng ching at no time can be broken. If you break this force you will become unstable with poor balance. Then a gap will occur which the opponent can take advantage of.

The bow is opened from the spine, then the arrow is released with dexterity and the strike comes from the spine. This is called strength striking from the spine. The strike comes from the center of the body. This is T'ai Chi boxing's theory of collecting and striking. In no other way can one borrow striking strength from the body. But, modern-day practice is different. Many people seem to conceal this striking power inside and not release it. They want to demonstrate elegance and refinement. If you practice like this for a long time, it is easy to train and not get the idea of striking energy. Then you will miss the point of practicing the set. Study and research this striking energy; is it or is it not drawing of silk and striking out? Do you have the idea of the arrow piercing the target? If you can grasp all three of these concepts, then you can say you have the proper T'ai Chi boxing striking energy.

Examples:

1. In Part the wild horse's mane, the strike is on the outside and upwards.

2. In Single whip step down, the strike is on the outside and downwards.

3. In Fair lady works at shuttles, the strike is on the inside and upwards.

4. In Deflect downward, parry, and punch, the strike is on the inside and in the center.

5. In Downward fist, the strike is also on the inside and in the center.

The above four categories of energy movement—"moving, receiving, collecting, and striking"—should be a standard for practice. These energies are unique to T'ai Chi boxing and are summarized as follows:

1. **Moving energy**   is the skill of change.
2. **Receiving energy**   is the skill of sticking.
3. **Collecting energy**   is the skill of pulling.
4. **Striking energy**   is the skill of attack.

Do not be lacking in any of these four categories. These are the basics. If the receiving energy is not good, then the moving energy will not be continuous, connected, and threaded together. If the moving energy is not connected and lacks Peng ching, then the collecting energy will not be able to roll. If you don't add flexibility to the collecting energy, then the strike cannot follow. This study is most important. This stage of development is the foundation of the T'ai Chi boxing skill. It is established. Don't worry if your skill is not improving. Take one step at a time, then another. This way you will make progress. Study every movement of the set.

Step Three: Study Following, Sinking, Lightness, and Dexterity

1. Following

The boxing chronicles say that the Ch'i moves the body. The body must move smoothly and easily in order to get an advantage in the skill of moving energy. It is very clear that it is from the revolving of drawing of silk, which must be smooth and easy going in or out. This following is a connecting line between the left foot and right hand, or the right foot and left hand.

In order to function beyond the use of ordinary strength, you must study what seems inconvenient and then work to make it efficient. Do not be convex or concave; do not have breaks or be overextended. There should be no shortcomings in moving these two drawings of silk (in and out). This is fundamental. Be smooth and easy in moving the Ch'i, and afterwards the body can move and rotate as it wishes in any direction.

When doing the set, investigate all of the drawing of silk, out and in. Learn how the movements exchange. Study the outward and inward drawing of silk. Observe the entering, the retreating, and the left and right. Then if the body has a shortcoming, it is because it does not have Peng ching. Without Peng ching the drawing of silk is impeded. If it is impeded then you cannot turn the body or move smoothly and easily.

2. Lightness

The boxing chronicles say that when the spirit of vitality is aroused, you are never slow or late. It is said that the top of the head is held as though suspended from above. In other words, the top of the head has Peng ching and can raise the spirit of the whole body. If you lighten the movements and transfer the weight, it becomes easy to shift to any position. When collecting energy is used as you turn, you can be light. Then it is easy to know others but not easy for them to know you. You can draw out the opponent's energy, and when turning your spirit is lively. This is T'ai Chi boxing's foundation of the spirit of vitality. If you are not light, additional weight cannot be felt; and you can't sense the opponent's energy and changes. When skillful, you can follow men, and during striking or releasing the defect of pitting strength against strength will not occur.

When you practice the set, study everything concerning collecting energy. In obtaining lightness, be sure not to have the harmful defect of raising the body up. Then the top of the head will have Peng ching.

3. Sinking

The boxing chronicles say that the mind moves the Ch'i. Strive to sink. When you strike you must sink. Relaxation and tension are beamed toward one focus at a time because when you have the achievement of Ch'i kung, then the Peng ching will cause the Ch'i to be gathered into the bones, so dexterity results from this sinking of the weight to one side. This sinking is chiefly due to Peng ching. Peng ching is the master energy when the Ch'i receives the mind's command. The general term for the mind's spirit of vitality is "will power." The mind makes the Ch'i sink, and all of your behavior will have the achievement of sinking.

The kicks of T'ai Chi boxing test the use of lower Peng ching. The Tan T'ien takes the lead and makes the Ch'i suddenly descend. Listen for this sound. According to the boxing chronicles, if movement is needed below, it must begin at the top. If you intend to kick, you must first order the body to utilize upper-body Peng ching. In other words, if you intend to sink, the body must first be light. If you intend to be light, the body must first sink.

Test the idea of left, right, front, back, upper and lower Peng ching. Is there any deficiency? How can T'ai Chi boxing take a spherical shape? When practicing the set, investigate all of the movements. Do you have sinking when you strike? Are you relaxed or tense when the Ch'i sinks and you release and strike? Don't be blocked or rise up when you strike. Performed properly, this achievement is like releasing an arrow.

4. Dexterity

The boxing chronicles say that the mind and the Ch'i must be interchangeable for the practitioner to get dexterity. It means having liveliness. So it is said, change from "empty to solid" in all movements. Dexterity is the changing of empty and solid. When one first begins to practice T'ai Chi boxing, the movements are completely empty and completely solid. When the skill becomes greater, the empty and solid quality of the movements will become more subtle and hidden. Then theoretically the changes will be more lively.

In the first step, the feet must be clearly divided between empty and solid. You can attain awareness of the feet being empty and solid if you pay attention. In the second step, the empty and solid of the hands must be clearly distinguished. If the right hand is in the front, the right hand is solid. If the right hand goes to the back, then the left hand turns to the front. The solid is shifted to the left hand in the front. This is what is called dexterity. If you try to make the right hand solid at this point, it will be blocked. In the third step, the right hand and the right foot, and the left hand and left foot are empty and solid, respectively. So, in every place there is this one empty and one solid. This is the third category and the most difficult to practice.

If you can understand dexterity, then the wheel can turn according to your wish to sacrifice yourself to follow others. Sink then follow. This section is about the power of empty and solid. The hands have upper Peng ching, which turns to lower Peng ching and vice versa. This is called responding. When you have upper Peng, the foot is solid; when you have lower Peng, the foot is empty. This transfer of dexterity is rapid. When you practice the set, first study the step's changes, the foot going from empty to solid. Then study the hand's transference from empty to solid, and then the hand and foot transferring from empty to solid. If you have this balance of empty and solid everywhere, it can be said that you have "ascended the chariot."

These four qualities—following, sinking, lightness, and dexterity—are T'ai Chi boxing's highest achievement. You must progress in order of sequence. It is not easy to master this effect. During moving energy you can change an opponent's energy if you are smooth and easy. When you use receiving energy, it will be dexterous. Then whether left or right you meet him at the source. The movements are designed to "sacrifice yourself to follow the opponent." During collecting energy, you are light and can pull another's energy. During striking you can sink. Then you can strike your opponent's energy. This is the four ounces moving a thousand pounds.

So, when you practice the set and understand the first step, you can advance to the second step and practice until skillful. Then when it is ingrained, you can proceed to the third step and change the second step's energy. When you attain real dexterity you can consciously measure the opponent's energy level and qualifications. When you have this, then you will study Push hands to practice awareness energy and the interplay of the Yin and Yang. You will gain deep experience and become very familiar with others' responses and habits. Achieve the martial arts method. To have come this far it should be clear that the slow can overcome the fast; this is the principle of weakness overcoming strength.

Chapter Three

Investigating the Method of T'ai Chi Boxing's Push Hands

Step One: The Push Hands System of Awareness Energy

From the preceding account of the skillful practice of the set, you have arrived at the level of Push hands. Awareness energy is acquired through the practice of Push hands. Two people must practice this together, and this practice is very important. If your Push hands opponent does not have a high level of skill, then you will fall into bad habits. Get the best-qualified Push hands opponent in order to mutually refine and polish this art. Then you will move on to the higher level of the method.

You must practice Push hands in accordance with the sphere of the T'ai Chi boxing books or you should not Push hands. You cannot get this from drawings or photos. If you try to learn Push hands from pictures or an unqualified opponent, you will develop the defect of slipping hands, and the technique will not be effective. The rules for Push hands practice follow:

1. Open, Close, Yin, and Yang

T'ai Chi theory says that T'ai Chi was born from Wu Chi, and Wu Chi is the mother of Yin and Yang. When there is movement, Yin and Yang separate, and in stillness they recombine. Theory also says that this subtle reasoning is the foundation of T'ai Chi boxing. The idea is to contain stillness inside. If the Ch'i is peaceful and harmonious, then you can distinguish the opponent's energy. In stillness there is movement, then you can transfer the refined Ch'i to spirit and change the opponent's energy.

With movement, the Yin and Yang are separated. This is called opening, and it is outward drawing of silk; it is attack. When you are still and the Yin and Yang are combined, this is inward drawing of silk; it is defense. In all of the T'ai Chi movements, don't forget these two functions. In the use of opening and closing the body, you must implement the achievement of Yin and Yang. Inside you contain empty, solid, receiving, and releasing. One arrives at the level of using tension and relaxation. The two must strive to be corresponding and then you can change in any direction. If you do not fully understand Yin and Yang, regardless of how clever you are, it is of no use in this skill. The T'ai Chi is born of two ideas. Only if you adhere to the above category can you attain the function of Yin and Yang. Never be without this principle.

2. Adhere, Stick, Connect, and Follow

Boxing theory says that you must utilize the movement of Yin and Yang. Use the opponent's posture to follow his form, and use the appropriate tool at the appropriate time. Then the light can overcome the heavy. It's all in the timing. The term "not arrive" means to get rid of defects. When you "arrive" you have sticking energy.

The term "not passing" refers to having light energy. To "follow the bent" is moving energy. If you cannot bend, then you have the defect of stiffness. To "follow the stretched" is following energy. If you expand to excess, then there is the defect of resistance. These four uses of energy are only learned through the practice of Push hands. There is no other way to get the actual use. You must complement these skills with the qualities of categories three and four, below.

3. Hard and Soft

Shifting between hard and soft smoothly and easily. T'ai Chi theory says that if an opponent is hard, I am soft. This is called evading. I follow the opponent's back and it is called adhering. When his strength comes toward me, I respond softly. Soft and hard dwell together. During soft energy you must especially conceal Peng ching. Don't forget the top of the head, then you can evade. If you are soft without Peng ching and attempt to become hard, the movements will be stiff. This cannot be called evading. If you can change from hard to soft in a smooth and easy manner, you can limit someone who is not smooth and easy. The person is drained of his power. To adhere is to attack; it is hard. Evading is the defense; it is soft. Evading is called draining energy, and adhering is called replenishing energy. When a man possesses this adhering and evading energy, then he can regulate the opponent's energy. After the skill of adhering and evading is acquired, the opponent's energy can be felt or intuited.

4. Quick, Slow, Adhering, and Evading

T'ai Chi boxing theory says that when the movement is quick, then respond quickly. If the movement is slow, then slowly follow. Although you use evading to draw someone in, adhering is used to break the opponent's root or balance. The opponent's motion must be followed whether it is fast or slow.

So, if the movement is fast, then respond fast. If the movement is slow, then slowly follow. When you have this achievement of responding with the appropriate speed, the quick and slow support each other. This is the way to feel the opponent's changes between motion and stillness. Examine these four categories when you practice. If you are not in the habit of using Open, Close, Yin, and Yang to move energy, then you can't judge the degree of fast and slow motion because you have not learned to distinguish the hard and soft. When you Push hands, also pay attention to Adhere, Stick, Connect, and Follow, and the smooth and easy change from soft to hard. How can you expect to correctly use T'ai Chi boxing if you can't distinguish Adhere, Stick, Connect, and Follow, or if you don't get the essence of Adhere and Evade?

In order to receive this awareness energy, you must do what is required, which is to Push hands for a long period of time and gain deep experience. Afterwards, the real Adhere, Stick, Connect, and Follow can be born. This is learning T'ai Chi boxing. You cannot excel without this stage of practice. Although the category of Adhere and Evade has many facets and complications, the principle is as stated. You must Push hands to maturity and gradually comprehend this awareness energy. From this awareness energy you can attain the class of the Gods. To avoid using strength takes a long time, and it is not possible to understand it suddenly. This is to learn Push hands, and the process of learning awareness energy. Study and research the above four steps.

Questions:

1. Do you have opening and closing energy in all of your movements? Do you have outward and inward drawing of silk?

2. Are Yin and Yang clearly distinguished in all movements? Are empty and solid clearly distinguished?

3. Do you have fast and slow power in all movements? Can you move between fast and slow smoothly and easily?

Step Two: The Posture and Force of Adhere, Stick, Connect, and Follow

1. Lightness

T'ai Chi boxing theory says that empty and solid energy are also at the top of the head. You must have lightness and dexterity in order to utilize Adhere, Stick, Connect, and Follow. After achieving lightness, you can know the heavy. The energy of the top of the head is empty and suspended. It is said that the top of the head has Peng ching. This is when the spirit of vitality is aroused. Then you won't have to worry about being slow or heavy, and the changes will be natural and lively.

2. Sinking

Boxing theory says that the Ch'i sinks to the Tan T'ien. In order to Adhere, Stick, Connect, and Follow, you must have the ability to sink. After sinking is understood, you can overcome opponents and not be overcome. Make the Ch'i sink to the Tan T'ien. This is the power of lower Peng ching. The mind moves the Ch'i, then you must sink and get the Ch'i to penetrate into the bones. Then when you push hands, you won't just be blown by the wind.

3. Upright and not leaning

Boxing theory says that to achieve this Adhere, Stick, Connect, and Follow you must not lean or incline. Your body must have the power of being upright, then you can sustain an attack from any direction. This upright body will provide you with a good position, enabling you to deal with all circumstances. This way a rigid posture won't be your downfall.

4. Don't lean on, don't sink into

T'ai Chi boxing theory says that if you want to Adhere, Stick, Connect, and Follow it is harmful to lean against an opponent's body or allow him to lean against you. This is important in learning awareness energy. Also, if the body rises up, then the root is broken. So you draw in the opponent but do not let him lean.

5. Dexterity

T'ai Chi boxing theory says "suddenly conceal, suddenly manifest." In order to use Adhere, Stick, Connect, and Follow, you must have the power of dexterity and liveliness. When you conceal you are soft and light. When you manifest you are hard and sinking. You can interchange soft and hard, lightness and sinking. Your dexterity is rapid. Opponents can't measure you, yet it is extremely easy to understand their methods.

The above five categories must be understood. Relaxation and tension are only focused on one thing at a time. Later, the two shoulders will each have a different purpose at the same time. If the left is heavy, then the right is light. If the right is heavy, then the left is light. This is the power of dexterity. If the opponent leans back, then you adhere high. If he leans towards you, then stick deep. If the opponent enters, then make the connection long. If he retreats, then closely follow. Attain this power. This is the consciousness of dexterity. A feather cannot be added without the body coming to life. Even a fly landing on the body will set it in motion.

Boxing theory also says that "Men do not know me, I alone know men." A hero is without peer because of this, because of learning Push hands. Study and research this second step.

Questions:

1. Does the dexterity rise to the top? Is the top suspended?
2. Is the Ch'i sunk to the Tan T'ien?
3. Is the body upright and not leaning?
4. Is there the defect of leaning against the opponent?
5. Is there a smooth and easy transfer from hard to soft? From lightness to sinking?

If you have the above categories mastered without defects, then you have the proper posture of Push hands. You can say that you have the spirit of vitality. Adhere, Stick, Connect, and Follow. Don't worry if this achievement does not happen right away. Seek out the awareness energy and you can prevail over other systems.

Step Three: Seeking Awareness Energy in Push Hands

1. Balancing energy

T'ai Chi boxing theory says that in order to seek out awareness energy, the body must stand like a scale. The top of the head is the top of the scale. The two hands at the left and right are the weighing plates. The two shoulders linked together form the scale's horizontal beam. The waist is the scale's root and the sacrum is the base of the upright post, threaded from the sacrum to the top of the head in a straight line. When the body stands like a scale, it can weigh the opponent's energy—whether it is great or small, light or heavy, rising or sinking. Everything is manifested in this scale. This is called the light and heavy method of awareness energy.

2. Neutralizing energy

T'ai Chi boxing theory says be lively like a wheel. Seek awareness energy. Although the body is like a scale, the wheel still needs to be installed. You need to think of measuring an opponent yet not being measured. You must measure and follow. The Ch'i must move the wheel. The waist is the axle, the two shoulders joined together wait, and the wheel moves horizontally side to side. The wheel moves in an erect position. One touch from any direction and it turns. This is how to get the measurement. This is called the directional method of awareness energy.

3. Pulling and attracting

T'ai Chi boxing theory says to sink to one side and follow. If your body is double-weighted, then it is impeded. Use awareness energy to know the opponent's direction—whether it is coming or going, or whether it is light or heavy, and to what degree. If you can do this, then you have the method of awareness energy. The body stands like a scale, not leaning. Also, it is lively like a wheel.

If the opponent adds strength in any direction, then you feel the sinking of your weight on one side in the direction of the movement. This is to "sacrifice yourself to follow the opponent." If the energy comes in, then the wheel revolves and you can draw in the opponent. If the energy goes away from you, then pull and four ounces can topple a thousand pounds. This pulling energy is very important in learning Push hands. The parent of pulling energy is the power of sinking on one side. If the opponent adds strength, you must adjust the sinking on that side. Then the body can revolve. This action of the wheel is hidden in the sinking of one side of your body. This hidden and uneven sinking can be to the left, right, up, down, front, or back, and the wheel will drag as it revolves. If you try to form the wheel at the left, right, front, or back with equal weight on both feet, you will have the defect of double-weightedness. Equal weight will impede the wheel and the body won't be able to move. If you lean past the balance point, the wheel will be toppled. You can measure another's energy level by this sinking on one side. Note that this is a hidden leaning.

The above three categories comprise the method of awareness energy. The body must be like a scale and a wheel simultaneously. The pulling action lends impetus to the movements. Boxing classics say that you may study for many years to gain this awareness and power, but if you have not corrected the defect of double-weightedness., you still cannot prevail over an opponent. To avoid this defect you must know Yin and Yang as well as the dexterity, solidity, lightness, and sinking, and the theory of reversal. You also must know how to adhere and evade. The hard and soft changes must be smooth and easy. When you have mastered these flowing changes, then adhering is evading and evading is adhering. Yin does not leave Yang, and Yang does not leave Yin. Evading and adhering are actually one response. Yin and Yang are combined. This is called awareness energy. When awareness energy is understood, the more you practice, the more refined you become. Gradually you can do what you intend.

Learn the steps of Push hands and study the following:

1. Does the scale feel the strength and weakness of the opponent? Can you distinguish it inside?

2. Outside, you have the wheel's rubber band; inside, is the degree of Ch'i enough?

3. When pulling, does it follow your intentions? Is it lively when changing from light to sinking?

4. Is your mental concentration good? Is dexterity never awkward or forced?

If you can answer yes to the above and fulfill the requirements of high-quality T'ai Chi, then you have the achievement of awareness energy. From this you can be sure of success. When this energy is understood, the body can follow in any direction that is required. You can strike without effort. From awareness energy alone it becomes possible to "sacrifice yourself to follow others."

When following others, you are in control, but if you follow blindly it has no effect. When following there must be a fixed spot to follow. Following can't be effected without knowledge. Respond from the nearest point to yourself and adhere. After you adhere to this point you turn and there is no escape for the opponent. Then follow, and regardless of how the opponent changes, adhere to this point's center of gravity. Follow one point not two. Follow closely, because if you do your body can become a lever. Then it is easy to get the opportunity and position of boxing. If one point is followed, then you won't grasp at shadows and miss the opponent. This is to seek awareness energy. This is understood from paying proper attention to adhere and evade. Most men can't function close in. T'ai Chi boxing theory says the foundation of this boxing method is to sacrifice yourself to follow the opponent. This is the ultimate conclusion of the T'ai Chi boxing theory. Learn to respond with extreme attention and focus. When you practice, ask yourself questions and discern the answers.

For reference, the study of the above three steps is for Push hands. Study and research these main points as the foundation of this exercise. It is imperative that you know Adhere, Stick, Connect, and Follow without the defect of leaning or inclining. If you fall short in any way, the movements are less than skillful.

Study Chart of Strengths and Weaknesses

Body	(strength)	Is it upright and comfortable?
	(weakness)	Are you looking up or down, slanting or inclining?
Form	(strength)	Is it lively and concentrated?
	(weakness)	Is it dull or lacking in insight?
Waist	(strength)	Is it like the wheel with the great banner-flag pole?
	(weakness)	Is it wooden or stiff like a stick?
Balance	(strength)	Is it complete, do you have dexterity?
	(weakness)	Is the Peng ching ever broken?
The wheel	(strength)	Can it move up or down, to the left and right, freely and unhindered?
	(weakness)	Does the wheel move too slowly? Is it impeded?
Pulling	(strength)	Does it have the hidden sinking on one side?
	(weakness)	Does it have the defect of being slow or heavy?

For reference the study of the above three steps is for Push hands. Study and research these main points as the foundation of this exercise. It is imperative that you know Adhere, Stick, Connect, and Follow without the defect of leaning or inclining. If you fall short in any way, the movements are less than skillful.

Chapter Four

The Energies of the Eight Gates and Five Steps

The "eight gates and five steps" refers to every category of energy for application in T'ai Chi boxing. Moving, Receiving, Collecting, and Striking are the most important. These four categories are for application in the art of defense and are the basic energies of the body. When you apply these energies, the direction will vary. Every one of these energies must be clearly distinguished.

According to the T'ai Chi boxing theory of Push hands, there are two basic energies. They are adhere and evade. They are all-encompassing. Adhere is to attack, and evade is to defend. In the doing of adhere and evade, they must be completely distinguished.

The boxing chronicles discuss the eight gates and five steps. The chief energies are the four primary hands,. and the four corner hands are for assistance. These eight gates represent the directions of energy, and the five steps represent the directions of the feet. The divisions are clarified as follows and will be addressed many times in the text.

The Energies of the Eight Gates Clearly Defined

1. Peng ching

Peng ching is the source of these eight methods. When you Push hands or practice the set, at no time can you neglect this category of energy. Actually, one can say that T'ai Chi boxing is Peng ching boxing because without Peng ching there is no T'ai Chi boxing.

Peng ching is the power of resilience and flexibility. It is born in the thighs and called Ch'i kung. Ch'i kung is concealed throughout the entire body. Then the body becomes the wheel's rubber band and you can gain the achievement of defense. But this is not the striking aspect. When you have this reaction force, you then have the ability to strike by returning the strike to its originator. This is the energy of defensive attack. It is used to evade and also to adhere.

When moving, receiving, collecting, and striking, Peng ching is always used. It is not easy to complete consecutive movements and string them together without flexibility. Peng ching is T'ai Chi boxing's essential energy. The body becomes like a spring; when pressed it recoils immediately.

2. Lu ching

This is Peng ching with a reverse direction. You can also call it Peng ching but Peng ching occupies the upper area towards the outside of the circle, and Lu ching occupies the lower area towards the inside of the circle. When you use Peng ching, your hand more often than not is under the opponent's hand. When Lu ching is used, your hand is usuallly on top of the opponent's hand.

Peng changes to Lu and is called inward drawing of silk. Lu changes to Peng and becomes outward drawing of silk. The two energies of Peng and Lu can at any time be interchanged. The Lu must also have Peng or it will not pull the opponent's body into your body. So, when moving, receiving, collecting, and striking, remember that the greater part of Lu is in collecting.

When your skill becomes deeper, then the energy of Peng and Lu can interchange in more subtle ways. When you see them, it is not easy to distinguish the changes of Peng and Lu because they can interchange at any instant. Peng ching contains the idea of attack and Lu ching contains the idea of defense. The separation of attack and defense becomes smaller and smaller, and then you get the most effective results because in attack there is defense, and in defense there is attack. This is the interaction of adhere and evade, the achievement of Yin and Yang working together.

3. Chi ching

This is often called "pressing." Chi is a supporting force that is used when there is not enough Peng ching. It relies on use of the two hands when they are joined. It can be said that this is a uniting energy. It focuses the energy of a pair of hands. It is two energies synthesized as one—the energy of dexterity.

Then Peng ching's thermometer is added, which is an energy to defend the chest. When this energy is close, it is attack and Tsai ching. It is the preparation of Tsai ching and is also Chi ching. It causes the two hands to defend securely. This energy can be Peng or it can be Lu. It is T'ai Chi boxing's energy of connecting attack and defense. But in Lu's method of use, both hands have Peng ching. From the use of the scale, one gets the successful use of the wheel and can revolve unhindered. Then the changes have dexterity. If one hand has Peng and one does not, it is easy to have the defect of leaning or inclining, and when revolving the changes will be slow.

4. An Ching

An ching is used as a listening energy. It is like having troops ready to move but holding them back until the command. It is listening for the opponent's changes. This energy is lower Peng ching and its use is in sinking. When sinking, the pulling force is created, which makes the opponent's base rise up. If An is from the front, then you revolve and use Peng ching. If it is from the left or right, you revolve and it is Lu ching. If An is combined, it becomes Chi ching and is actually releasing energy.

Within An ching is concealed the use of the fingers and T'ai Chi boxing's capturing and grabbing techniques. There is single An and double An. The palm and fingers are the chief players. Contained in the palm and fingers is Tsai ching's use, which will automatically change the other three energies.

The boxing chronicles say Peng, Lu, Chi, and An—you should spend a great deal of time to attain the real skill. When you can follow the up and down of the opponent, he has difficulty attacking you. These four characters are called the primary hands. They each have a reciprocal use. The changes from open to close and tight to loose are just a tiny revolving motion, but inside the energy changes.

To sum this up, Peng and Lu are for evading. Chi and An are for adhering. Usually Peng is moving energy and Lu is collecting energy. Usually Chi is receiving energy, and An more often than not is striking energy.

It is the boxing chronicle's rule that in the use of the four primary hands, everything occurs inside of the circle. You stand in a good position, and this positioning is T'ai Chi boxing's theme. Most people don't know how to think out their position when they encounter an opponent. The hand method is a great opening and a great closing. You are not trying to get rid of the opponent, yet you are not advancing.

When using this method, there can sometimes be difficulty and you can be forced to the outside of the circle. If you arrive at the outside of the circle, then you cannot use the four primary hands. An aid is needed; it is a vacant space and it is your opportunity. In this vacant space you must turn and attack. Get rid of the harm and receive the advantage. In this circumstance, the four corner hands must be used for aiding and repairing the four primary hands. This will return the body to a good position. The four corner hands are Tsai, Lieh, Chou, and K'ao. They are distinguished as follows:

5. Tsai ching

Tsai is reversing the direction of Chi ching. The idea of the hand on the outside is Peng, and the hand below is Tsai. It is like picking fruit—grabbing a branch and pulling the fruit off. When Tsai is used, you must draw silk towards the back and incline downwards. This is T'ai Chi boxing's grasping art and resides completely in the fingers. If the grasping technique is not practiced, you will not easily become skilled in the use of Tsai ching. You especially must have the outside Peng in order to keep the two hands in balance. If the opponent gets the concept of the Tsai hand, the hand with Peng will naturally adhere and prevent his escape. Then one utilizes the corner hands in support of the primary hands.

When using Tsai, do not pull against the opponent's will. You must revolve and afterwards use Tsai. Also, don't use Tsai horizontally towards the back; it must incline downwards towards the rear. This will uproot the opponent.

6. Lieh ching

Lieh is the chief striking energy but differs from releasing energy. When you strike it is not directly at the body. You encounter a vacant space or gap between yourself and the opponent to use Lieh's strike. Don't measure or wait for a reaction. When Lieh is used, one hand has Lieh and the other hand must have inside drawing of silk energy in order to keep the body's balance in any direction. The hands mutually interchange their use.

If the opponent is concerned about his hand going out of the circle or being overextended, then Lieh's strike can be used. If the opponent reacts to the hand with Lieh's energy, then the other hand has the rolling and releasing effect which will return you to equilibrium. This is the method of the corner hand supporting the primary hand. Lieh's use is to draw silk outward towards the opponent when you are very close. This is also called T'ai Chi boxing's small strike energy. When the strike's energy is first released, you cannot stop halfway and change. You are committed and it is not always a safe way. So, T'ai Chi boxing's Lieh energy strike is done quickly and begins a few inches away from the opponent's body.

7. Chou ching

Chou is the strike's second line of defense. When you are overextended or outside the circle and Tsai and Lieh don't work, then it is time to use Chou. When you are overextended and can't get a good position, you are vulnerable and can't stop the directions of your arms. Then the opponent can pull you and it becomes force against force. If you just struggle with muscle against muscle to regain your equilibrium, how can you call this the light overcoming the heavy? During this situation, use Chou's energy because you can transfer the energy from the wrist to the elbow. Chou's elbow strike is used inside of the circle and close in. From this you can again return to central equilibrium. Once again the corner hand supports the primary hand.

8. K'ao ching

K'ao's strike is the third line of defense. When Chou is used and you find yourself outside of the circle or overextended, or during double Peng when the arms are tied up and you can't return to central equilibrium, K'ao must then be used. However, you can't continue to go forward in a straight line. You can't give the opponent the opportunity to use connecting energy or recover his balance. Therefore, you use K'ao in a slanting direction so the opponent cannot recover. At the upper part of your body you use shoulder K'ao, towards the lower part of the body you use knee K'ao. You strike like a hinge. If you are right against a person's face you use stomach K'ao. If your body is turned around then use back K'ao. K'ao's use is that of the body striking when the arms and feet are tied up. K'ao also fills the vacant space between two people. It is another instance of the corner hand supporting the primary hand.

When you practice the T'ai Chi boxing set and progress in its skill, the empty and solid deviations become more and more hidden. The inner energy is transferred more easily and the movements utilize smaller circles. This change greatly affects your dexterity. When you meet an opponent's energy, the sinking changes to half light and half heavy. These changes are complex, and if you are not completely cautious, then you can run into the danger of being overextended—in other words, going outside of the circle. However, the foot method can be used to rectify this undesirable situation. In such instances, if the corner is not available to use, you can move swiftly and expediently with the foot method.

The corner hand is not restricted to supporting the four primary hands, but also has the power to defeat opponents. One character, two uses. The corner hand has proven its high rank. The corner hands Tsai and Lieh are used to stop the opponent's wild action. But you must use adhere and stick first to support the primary hands. If you are using the corner hands of Chou and K'ao, it is because you have become overextended while using Tsai and Lieh and there is no way to turn back.

In T'ai Chi boxing, the four primary hands are the basic rule and the four corner hands are the alternatives. They provide the power to keep going. These are the rules, and you must devote yourself to improvement to understand them. When you grasp the use of the eight gates, the primary hands become more and more manifest, and the corner hands become ever more concealed. You cannot often use the corner hands, but one must become skillful in their use. The corner hands support the primary hands because you don't show them until the opportunity arises, and then they suddenly appear. This is the best strategy. Combine these two ideas. When you perform a complete set of T'ai Chi boxing, at no time can you be without Peng ching. If you are without Peng ching then you have the defect of not being connected. Lu is inside and lower Peng. Chi is reversing Peng's uniting energy; An is lower Peng and also front Peng. There is no way to give examples of the primary hands because the variations are too numerous. If you investigate the set's corner hands, you will only find eighteen of them. The examples of the set's corner hands are as follows:

Tsai ching

Carry tiger hand is revolving Tsai.

Part the mane hand is diagonal Tsai.

Repulse the monkey is divided Tsai.

High pat on horse is double Tsai.

Lieh ching

Deflect, parry, and punch is revolving Lieh.

Turn and kick is foot Lieh.

Finger block punch is diagonal Lieh.

Downward fist is lower Lieh.

Step up to form seven stars is combined Lieh.

Lady works at shuttles is lifting Lieh.

Shoot tiger is circular Lieh.

Separate foot is sharp Lieh.

Cross wave kick is foot direction Lieh.

Cross wave of water lily is sweeping Lieh.

Chou ching

Fist under elbow is Yin Chou.

Strike tiger force is horizontal Chou.

K'ao ching

Slanting flying force is diagonal K'ao.
Cloud hands is horizontal K'ao.

Investigate the above movements. They are the corner hands. Many popular sets want to express elegance and use less corner hands. This way the energy is hidden and not used. No wonder that people think that T'ai Chi boxing is not a martial art. When you practice and don't really strike, how can you get the martial arts aspect? Practice is not being on a stage to entertain people. If you do not pass through this practice, how can you know how to strike from no practice?

We must question persistently. Although one practices profoundly, if the corner hands are avoided and only the primary hands are used, this is a shortcoming. When two people compete with each other, it is difficult to avoid overextending. If the corner hands are not prepared to remedy the situation, how can the missed force be restored and returned to equilibrium?

The boxing classics say: "Tsai, Lieh, Chou, and K'ao, alternate and win by surprise." If you practice T'ai Chi boxing from beginning to end and do not pay attention to the corner hands, there will be regrets. The past generations of the Ch'en family felt that the corner hands contained in the first form were too few, so another set was created in which use of the corner hands was the main theme. The primary hands were not as pronounced in this form.

The Five Steps Clearly Divided

The steps are the root of the body. Flexibility comes from the knees. Boxing classics say that to get the opportunity and position of boxing, the waist and thighs must be studied. The knee is the principle. If your strides are not favorable, it is because the steps are not proper. So, the step method influences the power of the whole body by the quality of the steps. In all movements, dexterity comes from the body, and the body has its root in the feet.

Enter, retreat, left, right, and center are the five basic changes. Depend on the steps to follow the body and then the changes will be lively. The five steps are positioned for drawing silk and used for receiving and releasing energy. The steps are divided into fourteen steps as explained below.

1. Breaking step

This method of stepping is found only in T'ai Chi boxing. It is generally directed towards the front. The heel is stuck to the ground, and the thigh and knee are curved and collecting. The toe rises. When this step is used in T'ai Chi boxing it is a benefit, but in other boxing arts this step is a defect because this step is more agile and can contract more easily and quickly. Other martial arts do not have this concept of yielding.

In T'ai Chi boxing, the basic rule is that "to enter is to be born and to retreat is to die." In other words, you rarely retreat because it is not necessary. The body contains the idea of the scale and uses the revolving of the wheel. Don't pit muscle against muscle; therefore to enter and not retreat is the best way. Even so, you sometimes have to withdraw a little, but only in preparation for advance.

The hands have Peng ching, and a circular energy is used to alter the opponent's position. Once you stretch out with this breaking step, you can sink and it becomes easy to revolve. When you revolve, the toe comes up; when you contract, the toe comes down and then you can strike. Use this special step as a rule. One example is Brush knee and twist step.

2. Backward breaking step

In all of the T'ai Chi boxing movements, only Repulse the monkey has the backward breaking step. The toe settles first and the rest of the foot settles afterwards. It is like the Breaking step but in the reverse direction.

3. Rolling step

In general, when you revolve to the left or right in T'ai Chi boxing, the foot sticks to the ground after it follows the body and then revolves to the left or right. This way you don't have the problem of inclining forward or leaning backward, so it is called the Rolling step. The sole of the shoe creates friction when it rolls on the ground. Examples include Deflect, parry, and punch, Strike tiger, and others.

This step can follow the changes of the body because it can roll to the left or right. The Rolling step can follow the body's turns to enable you to sacrifice yourself to follow the opponent. The whole body can remain comfortable and the movements can all be strung together. The Breaking step and Rolling step are the foundation of T'ai Chi boxing's foot strategy. When you Move, Receive, Collect, and Strike never forget these two steps.

4. Rising step

This step uses the force of one leg rising. It trains the thigh's upper Peng ching, requiring the thigh to move in a circular way. One example is Golden cock stands on one leg.

5. Sinking step

This is a way of raising one's thigh and putting it back down. It trains the thigh's lower Peng ching. When the thigh is lowered it still contains the idea of circular motion. An example is the Ch'en family's intersecting step. This step is mostly forgotten.

6. Withdrawing step

This step opens from the inside to the outside. The thigh is circular and when open contains Peng ching. Carry tiger to mountain is an example. This step is a left or right withdrawal.

7. Collecting step

This step is done from the outside towards the inside. The thigh must have circular form and have Lu ching. The up and down must be blended as in Cross wave hand and others.

8. Curved step

This is the outside drawing of silk step. It is used for attack or defense as in Part the wild horse's mane.

9. Slanting step

This is when the step shifts diagonally to the left or right. The upper and lower body parts must be blended and the step can move forward or backward as in Diagonal single whip.

10. Horse riding step

This has the form of someone riding a horse and is a double sinking step. It has double Peng ching. An example is Single whip and there are others.

11. Fishing step

This is the Horse riding step moving to the left or right. The thigh and hand circulate and support each other. An example is Cloud hand and there are others.

12. Fairy step

This is when the top of the body rises and the inside receives. The point of the toe is placed on the ground as in White stork cools its wings and others.

13. Turn the body over step

This involves placing the spine in a position to revolve for striking. The thighs must have outward and inward drawing of silk. An example is Chop opponent punch.

14. Pushing step → 'L?' has PUSHING STEP

The front step is taken and the back foot follows the front. The thigh has forward Peng ching energy; it turns and pushes. An example is Apparent close up, and there are others.

For historical interest there are other steps, such as: Falling flower step, Reverse riding deer step, Chasing step, The belt hits step, Divided body step, and the Threaded loom step.

T'ai Chi boxing's steps often contain two of the above energies at once, so it is not easy to state clearly which step is which energy. When you enter towards the front, this also contains energy from the left and right, and so the five main steps are generally referred to as the five steps—enter, retreat, left, right, and center. This designates the boxing art's footwork.

During ancient times the student's mentality was shaped by ideas from the Pa Kua-Wu Hsing era. In fact, the eight energies were divided inwardly. How can you explain the eight gates and the five directions of the steps? One should recognize T'ai Chi boxing as one family because in this boxing art there is always a mutual relationship between the Pa Kua and the Wu Hsing. The

Pa Kua and Wu Hsing are combined to form this school of T'ai Chi boxing.

If you study T'ai Chi boxing's steps, you will see that the rolling step is the foundation of neutralizing energy, and the breaking step is the method of frontal attack. The object of these steps is a rapid change of direction. If you use the breaking step as an attack, the body must move like a cat. Empty stride out and solid when you release. If the thigh is lifted too high, it will cause the rest of the body to rise. If the foot scrapes the ground when you enter, the movement will be blocked. If your intention is not to rise up or be blocked, then the foot method must contain sinking and liveliness. But these two are not easy to unite. If you want to be lively, then it's not easy to sink. If you want to sink, then it is not easy to be lively. But using the T'ai Chi boxing principles, both must be implemented at the same time. Then the foot method will be understood completely. T'ai Chi boxing's steps have specialized rules that are combined for a specialized purpose:

1. T'ai Chi boxing's steps must have Peng ching when the stride releases in order for the hand to open and release. The intersecting drawing of silk motion is endless and unbroken. Then there will be no shortcomings.

2. T'ai Chi boxing's steps are catalyzed by the motion of the hand. The foot moves to follow the hand. The hand and foot movements correspond and are one in their effectiveness.

3. While releasing, T'ai Chi boxing's steps should sink in the foot which is under the hand, and the hand must have upper Peng. This is how the upper and lower are interrelated and work together.

In accordance with the above rules, T'ai Chi boxing's steps are organized by the hand. The hand also has to sink down to get Peng ching's foundation. If the thigh has Peng ching, then you will know lightness and dexterity. Although there is lightness, it is still not enough for martial use. You especially must have sinking. You must stick to the ground and move in order to get the relationship between lightness and sinking. Then the stride is stuck to the ground and can develop great energy. If you understand this posture then you have T'ai Chi boxing's special step method. During the combining of lightness and sinking, you have to pull out Peng ching in order to really achieve this and understand the relationship of the top and bottom of the body. Be glad to learn this boxing and the moving energy of the steps. Especially give deep thought to assigning names to the steps to further your awareness.

The Practice of the Set and its Representation of the Eight Gates and the Five Steps

You will become skilled only as a result of intense study and by forging T'ai Chi boxing's method. The movements of the set's structure must be analyzed so that every motion, every energy can be clearly distinguished. One after another, study them all until your knowledge is complete. Then you will have the skill to respond to any opponent. If you don't pay particular attention to the lively motion of the set, and don't distinguish the inside energy, then the set has no meaning and is merely an empty form.

How can you increase your skill? Although you may practice a great deal, don't avoid the real challenges. In order to really practice this boxing you must know every category of the set. The four primary hands and the four corner hands are the main points. You must completely understand the eight methods or "gates" and dedicate yourself to progress or you will have a weakness. If you don't know the fast and the slow, if the hard and the soft are not distinguished, if the light and the heavy are not divided, how can you receive the achievement of the eight methods? Without this achievement Push hands has no meaning.

Push hands is the way you achieve the eight methods by experimentation. From this lively action results are produced and proven. The set is the foundation; Push hands is its use. If you are skillful at performing the set, have you really touched upon its use? Once you arm the soldiers, are they really prepared to prevail on the battlefield? Today the T'ai Chi boxing forms have many styles, yet they all uphold the same principle. No one can create his own school of T'ai Chi boxing because the essence of this boxing is the eight methods and five steps. It is impossible to deviate from this principle and create a separate school of T'ai Chi boxing. Regardless of the school or set your practice is from, by using the eight methods which have been fully perfected your skill can increase. The outside becomes manifest and the inside becomes concealed. You can't surpass this achievement. So, regardless of the school of T'ai Chi boxing you adhere to, they all must follow the same rules when performing the sets. First apply the standards of the boxing classic "Kung Hsin Chieh" and then pursue your studies and remove any defects you may have. Again, examine the energies of ordinary movement and divide them into the eight methods and five steps. If you follow in accordance with real practice, you will act properly in all movements and will contain the idea within.

Chart of Energy Division

The following is an example from the chart translated into English.

Movement	Energies distinguished	Foot method
Single whip	Peng Lu K'ao and Lu An	Horse riding step
White stork cools its wings	horizontal Tsai and divided Peng	Fairy step
Brush knee twist step	Peng Lu and Peng An	Breaking step
Carry tiger hand	Peng Lu and then Tsai	Withdrawing step
Upper cloud hand	Peng Lu and Peng Lu	Fishing horse step
Lower cloud hand	Peng Lu and Lieh Lu	Fishing horse step

This chart was left behind by Mr. Ch'en Ch'ang Hsing as a representation of the original Ch'en family form. Through the generations it has not been modified, and that is why it remains a good example. Mr. Ch'en Ch'ang Hsing's legacy has been passed to the present day without interruption. His descendants were farmers, simple and honest people who were not so pretentious as to change the style the ancestors had left behind.

This chart which distinguishes the energies of the eight methods and five steps is complete in its identification of the energies and provides a handy reference. Only a small portion of it is given in English, but this alone can be used for study. Regardless of what school you are from, you can compose a similar chart of your own. Then the set will greatly increase in meaning and concept, and you can harbor this skill within yourself and continue to advance. Then the maximum results are received with less effort.

To fully understand this boxing, the foot method must be considered and given special attention, because the step is the root of the whole body. If the steps are good, the body will always find good circumstances. The foot method follows the action of the body. If the body follows the steps, then it is a defect. If the foot moves and the shoulders follow, then it is good. If the shoulders move and the foot follows, then it is a defect.

When the foot method is good, you don't have to force an action. It will come naturally. Then the upper and lower parts of the body work effectively as one unit. If the steps are not skilled, then all the movements come to nothing. In modern-day practice of this boxing, you often see people practice as though the upper body is T'ai Chi boxing and the lower body is not T'ai Chi boxing. This is detrimental. Look into the reason for the many steps and follow in accord with the principles.

Other boxing schools generally believe that the greater one's physical strength, the easier the victory. Defense is the main point, and that's why T'ai Chi boxing is also called the Post step. It means that you can stand in a fixed position without retreat. The lightness of the steps is a main point, and the sinking is its use. During a strike you can organize and interchange empty and solid to be completely connected. This is because the drawing of silk of the hand and foot allows the top and bottom of the body to form a whole. Other boxing methods are contrary to this method. If you only focus on the hand movements and do not calculate the drawing of silk of the steps, then you will achieve little result despite Herculean effort.

T'ai Chi Boxing's Chart of the Five Steps

enter forward	breaking step, pushing step, chasing step, connecting branch step
retreat backward	backward breaking step
looking left	rolling step, turn the body over step, withdrawing step, collecting.step, slanting step, curved step
looking right	rolling step, turn the body over step, withdrawing step, collecting step, curved step, slanting step
central equilibrium	rising step, horse riding step, fishing step, fairy step, falling flower step, divided body step

[handwritten annotations:] Follow & Connect · Adhere & Stick

The enter and retreat steps also have energy from the left and right. The left, right, and center steps have enter and retreat energy. Central equilibrium is the chief of the steps. The left and right steps are Adhere and Stick. The enter and retreat steps are Follow and Connect.

Chapter Five

The Sequence of Learning
T'ai Chi Boxing

In the general process of learning, the basis should be scientific. Many avenues must be explored in order to progress, and the practitioner should not be limited to just a corner or the perspective is incomplete. Do not skip the necessary progression by jumping from a low level to a high level and missing what is in between. The proper way is to learn gradually by building a solid foundation.

T'ai Chi boxing is a specialty and thus uses special principles that differ completely from other types of boxing. Don't stay in a corner with no change. In your progress from elementary school to the university, you did not use just one textbook to succeed. You also did not get from one point to another by skipping grades. Examine and study the skill of awareness energy because it is T'ai Chi boxing's graduation, the Ph.D. After you get this awareness energy, the more you practice, the more refined you become. Memorize and ponder, then gradually you will receive what you intend. Everyone's depth and attainment are different. The level which you can attain is of course limited by your intelligence and natural talents. But you can complete this Doctorate degree.

Thus, the goal of practice is to arrive at awareness energy. This is the Professorship. After you gain this awareness energy, you con-

tinue to listen and learn and personally realize yourself. When you
arrive at this high level you no longer need the rules, but again you
must ask to progress. Although you intend to educate others, there
is no way to explain the teaching you have received. Because of
your developed intuition, you can perceive spontaneously and not
through explanations. Although you can explain the essential points,
if the other person does not feel the achievement inside, then naturally he can't understand what you say. There is no way to give
proof. So, the progression of teaching reaches only to the thresh-
old of awareness energy. According to the boxing classics, awareness energy must be able to attract the entrance of the opponent
and then make his attempt fail. Adhere, Stick, Connect, and Follow are never disconnected from him. Without restriction, a great
force is intercepted and the pulling of four ounces topples a thousand pounds. On the surface, you see these four ounces but you
don't feel within how they are applied. Because the opponent's
energy is drawn towards you inside the circle, his attempt will fail.
The opponent's root is broken and his Ch'i is made to rise. Because
of the leaning/sinking of Adhere and Stick, the pulling of an opponents body uses four ounces of energy to topple over and raise the
root of a thousand pounds.

The words are very easy to understand; the doing is very difficult. From the time you first begin to study and enter the gate of
learning up to the attainment of comprehension, you need the
method to explain this line of forward entry. Afterwards, this line
is practiced. How can you proceed to the ultimate achievement?
According to the Lee family boxing chronicle, the stages of development are divided into nine parts as follows.

Part One: The Practice of the Set

You cannot learn the set without oral teaching, regardless of how
carefully you follow charts or graphs, even if every detail is included.
With this method the student will become more and more vague.
If you intend to learn the form of T'ai Chi boxing from a book, it

is really not possible. If you try to learn from movies, you can only pick up a little bit this way. But oral teaching will give the three-dimensional concept and the complete understanding of moving in the eight directions.

Currently there are many people who practice this boxing. If you are taught directly by a teacher, it will relieve you of concerns about practicing the set properly. When you enter the gate, rely on oral teaching; you waste time learning by yourself. There are three chief ingredients that a student must have to reach the plateau of boxing:

- You must encounter an excellent teacher and follow his method of instruction.
- You must be willing to spend time and have perseverance.
- You must be bright and have comprehension.

These three ingredients are all connected. The second and third ingredients are relative to the student's ability, so they cannot be demanded. The first ingredient is determined by whether you have the opportunity or can recognize the opportunity. The teacher must be skilled in passing down the system. The student should use the boxing classics as a standard before proceeding to receive instruction. This way after you take the course of action and are taught by a teacher, you will be able to rectify any shortcomings you may have developed. When the teacher makes a correction, it is easy for him to point out what movements are not up to standard. Piece by piece the whole form will be corrected and modified until it is completely correct. If this method is followed, you won't have the problem of getting it in the beginning and later forgetting.

Ch'en P'in San says: In the practice of T'ai Chi boxing, you have to take great care and think all matters through to their limit. If you don't do this you will lack common sense and in the end be ignorant. If you don't pay the greatest heed, you won't have the energy inside. You may think you are doing well but this might not be the case. Work with full effort from the beginning to the end without interruption in order to have a complete understanding. When the form has been corrected and is completely skillful, then you can progress to the second part.

Part Two: The Practice of Drawing Silk

Moving energy is the name of drawing silk. Among the drawing of silk motions you will invariably find outward and inward drawing. The outward extends away from the body, and the inward comes towards the inside. Opening and closing are the parents of outward and inward. From the outward and inward drawing of silk the energy of opening and closing is produced. When you use the set's inner energy you can never forget outward and inward in any movement or direction. There are many drawings of silk, divided for your identification and known together as the twelve drawings of silk.

In T'ai Chi's moving energy, you always use the twelve drawings of silk. If not, then the outward motion may look like round energy, but the inside energy remains straight. In this case you miss the idea of T'ai Chi boxing, and the achievement of the light overcoming the heavy is not realized. Drawing of silk's energy is T'ai Chi boxing's foundation. It is like the English alphabet. Regardless of whether you are a novice or an expert, you had better use this special practice. Like the alphabet forming words, this alphabet is for every strike or movement and the drawings of silk mutually support each other. This is the way to get the proper moving energy. Then not only is learning the set easier, but the job of the teacher is simplified because he can correct the defects inside the set. If you can learn the drawing of silk, then you can eradicate the defects from T'ai Chi boxing's moving energy. These defects include the following:

1. Head leaning forward
2. Top of the head leaning
3. Rising shoulders
4. Raised elbows

5. Hunchback

6. Concave chest

7. Unstable waist

8. Buttocks sticking out

9. Hips not aligned

10. Crotch sticking out

11. Straight knees

12. The bottom of the foot slanted

These are the twelve main defects. They occur during moving energy, and if you happen to have just one of these, the drawing of silk between the hand and foot is impeded. How can you achieve proper movement yet feel like you didn't move at all? This drawing of silk energy can be understood thoroughly by experimentation. If you can draw silk smoothly and easily, then the twelve defects naturally will not arise.

Examples of drawing silk:

1. Left right Cloud hands is left right following drawing of silk.

2. Left right Grasp the bird's tail is left right outward drawing of silk and right small inward drawing of silk.

3. Left right Part the wild horse's mane is left outside outward drawing of silk and right inside inward drawing of silk.

4. Left right Brush knee and twist step is left upper entering outward drawing of silk and right lower retreating inward drawing of silk.

5. Left right Strike tiger force is left large outside entering outward drawing of silk and right small inside lower retreating inward drawing of silk.

The Wang chronicle says: "The energy is severed, but the intention is not severed." If the intention is severed you cannot receive.

These writings say that receiving is releasing, releasing is receiving. Close and afterwards open. This means that in T'ai Chi boxing's receiving and releasing you do sever the energy and the connection. When you use this severing, the energy can still come out of the body and be returned to the opponent. If you don't sever, then the energy from the body cannot be called releasing. So, during receiving and releasing, when the greatest strength comes, then sever and you can return and connect. It is the achievement of receiving or joining energy.

The Wang chronicle also says that in all movements the whole body must be light and strung together without shortcomings. Don't be convex or concave. The movements should not be sporadic or intermittent. From the root at the foot to the supreme power of the waist, the energy is expressed in the fingers. From the base to the thighs to the waist, the movement must be intact and whole throughout the entire body. This way whether you move forward or back, you have the measurement and the force. This means that drawing silk's moving energy uses moving energy's drawing of silk. Observe the following:

1. Don't have shortcomings. This means means that from the feet to the fingers you are full of connected energy when drawing silk.

2. Don't be convex or concave, meaning that from the feet to the fingers the drawing of silk's curved line must be smooth and easy, and this line should not be abrupt or shaky.

3. Don't be intermittent or stop and go quickly. When you draw silk in or out from the foot to the fingers, you must endlessly revolve. Don't stop and start even when the outward drawing of silk becomes inward drawing of silk.

The above exchanges are called Turning energy, and if there is the problem of being intermittent then the body will not remain strung together. If strength is added under such circumstances the energy is wasted. Should this occur, one fails to realize the concept of the light prevailing.

In learning T'ai Chi boxing, the drawings of silk must be clearly distinguished. Observe whether they include this proper severing or continuing. The severing and continuing must be clearly divided. Their use is to sever and then follow and connect. It is important to get these two ideas of severing and continuing. If you have observed the rules in the second section, the drawings of silk will be complete and proper, and then you have received the real force of T'ai Chi boxing's form. After you get this drawing of silk, you can progress to the next step and ask for the skill of inner energy. T'ai Chi boxing applies the process of outward energy gathered inside.

Part Three: Learning to Separate the Energies

To learn the separation of energies, use the practice method of the eight gates and five steps. Although there are eight energies, the key is Peng ching. If Peng ching is drawn inside, then it is called Lu. If Peng is drawn down, then it is called An. Combined Peng is called Chi. Divided Peng including An is called Tsai. Peng followed by a strike is called Lieh. Peng turning and the elbow striking is called Chou. Peng turning and the body striking is called K'ao. All eight energies have their basis in Peng ching. On the surface Peng ching has different appearances so it is called the eight gates, but the root is always Peng ching. So to succeed in these three parts you must contain Peng ching.

In all movements and in every transition, Peng ching is the foundation of pulling out the inside force. There are strict rules governing flexibility in all movements. When the rules are understood then Peng ching will occur and the postures will be proper. Every joint of the body must be continuously strung together like a bamboo shoot with its segments or joints. You must string together the joints like the back of a bow, or picture the bamboo shoot bent like a bow and notice how all the joints evenly sustain the bend-

Lu ←Peng
↓
An

ing. If you intend to create the form of a bow's back in the body, then every joint must make a smoothly curved line. This is the energy of drawing silk's "revolving bow's back." To achieve this you must be in accordance with the following rules (presented in three points):

The first point

The two upper arms are connected above the elbow and below the shoulder. They are suspended in a line and embody the idea of reciprocal connection. When the two upper arms connect like this, then Peng ching is born; between the two upper arms there appears a bow or arc. The bow is flexible and its action consistently strung together. The rules of the arm bow are as follows:

1. The body must be centered, so that when the bow's back bends, the flexibility is equal on both sides.

2. The shoulders should sink, so the action of the bow's back is tightly connected to the spine. Thus when this arm bow is formed it has greater completion and strength.

3. The elbows should sink. This adds to the flexibility of the bow and sends the message to the hands through the joints.

4. The wrists should be straight. This causes the bow to be curved. If the wrists are not straight, then flexibility can't be passed down to the hands.

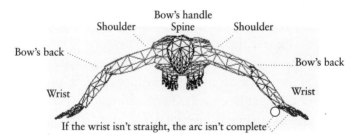

Bow's handle
Shoulder   Spine   Shoulder
Bow's back

Bow's back

Wrist   Wrist

If the wrist isn't straight, the arc isn't complete

Picture of the arm bow

The second point

The two thighs follow each other. When one thigh strides, the other must follow to support it and form the leg bow. Then Peng ching is born and the steps will be lively. The thighs are different from the hands. They can't produce Peng ching as easily as the arms, but if Peng ching is not produced in the legs, then there will be a defect. The hand motions differ from the foot motions because they can move faster and the up-and-down movements are easier to do. The revolving is done by the waist. Lightness and sinking are separated. When you step and one thigh is empty and one is solid, this forms the arc of the leg bow. The rules are as follows:

5. The buttocks should be tucked in. Then the leg bow can tightly connect with the center.

6. The knees should be bent. It increases the flexibility of the leg bow and the message can be sent to the spine.

7. The step should be light. This gives the leg bow the advantage of flexibility because from the light steps and the sinking down, the bow is opened.

8. The feet must be empty and solid. This gives the leg bow flexibility and reciprocally makes them weak and strong. If the leg bow is not divided into empty and solid then you cannot be lively. This is not like the arm bow which can turn very lightly.

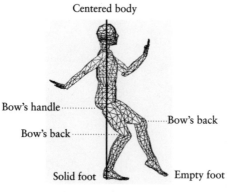

Picture of the leg bow

The third point

The back bow collects energy at the chest. This is a vertical bow which turns at the chest as a point of resistance. The back turns in order to pull the bow. The back bow is not as quick as the arm or leg bows. So, the chest contains the idea of collecting. The back revolves and pulls the bow back and creates collecting energy. The chest cannot be convex or concave. If the chest is concave, you can't revolve from the spine. If the back can't revolve, then it can't be said to contain collecting. This body bow is the main force of the arm and leg bows. The body must be held erect like a post. These three bows are very important. The rules are as follows:

9. The top of the head turns. This makes the upper end of the body vertical like a scale, and then the arm bow is proper and the leg bow lively.

10. The back must rotate. This gives the body bow great flexibility. The spine is the bow's back.

11. The waist must be tight. Use this to test the method of the body bow being straight up and down. If the waist is slanted or crooked then it can't be tight and connected.

12. The lower belly rises. It makes the front section of the body bow empty—similar to the tightness of the waist.

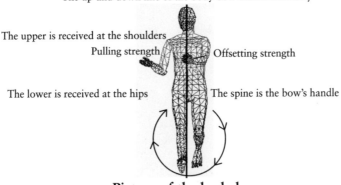

The up-and-down line of the body bow creates flexibility

The upper is received at the shoulders

Pulling strength

Offsetting strength

The lower is received at the hips

The spine is the bow's handle

Picture of the body bow

The numbered rules above are the foundation, and the three points are the use. These are the tools which create Peng ching. After long practice you will increase flexibility and have a complete concept of Peng. The above rules and points are the essentials of Peng ching. If you do not practice according to these principles, it will not be possible to master this concept. These principles apply in stillness as well as in movement. If these principles are fulfilled in all movements—then the up and down, the left and right, the enter and retreat, the inside and outside, the large and small, and the outward and inward—then the energy of the eight gates and five steps all will be contained within. Then you will have learned the separation of the energies.

Therefore, when you begin to learn T'ai Chi boxing it must be slow, and quickness should not be permitted so you can observe and study these three points and twelve rules. When you first begin to practice T'ai Chi boxing, you must have a teacher nearby to give you corrections or it will not be easy to understand these secrets. After you have received the proper kind of instruction your body will instantly feel whether you have Peng ching, and you will be able to correct your own bad habits. The above rules of the postures must be passed down by a teacher, and this is the only way to learn.

Peng ching is the root of flexibility and this root must be studied and examined in detail. When Peng ching is comprehended, then the Ch'i can be threaded and strung together inside to increase flexibility; you then can say it is real Peng ching. Peng ching's sole source is in the Ch'i, and the Ch'i is threaded together smoothly and freely to the joints, causing the whole body to be completely connected. In order to practice Ch'i, the posture must be correct and you must have the idea of Peng ching.

This section focuses on whether or not you have Peng ching, because Peng ching is the first indication of the Ch'i. All movements must be practiced and distinguished as parts of the whole and mastered before they can be united. For example, if you are wielding Peng and Lu, the upper part of Brush knee you receive from the head to the hand. The lower part will receive at the step and is Brush knee and twist step.

Everything cannot be practiced at the same time. If you try to just generally learn movements without specific knowledge, your set will not be polished. Boxing classics say: In all the actions you should first practice one action and practice it to maturity. Then practice it again before you connect the movements. Do not be impatient. The movements must be practiced one by one fully. Then you will naturally come to a full understanding. This practice is also called Ch'ang Ch'uan or long boxing. The execution of the set cannot have a polished foundation unless the student passes through this practice method. If the entire sphere of the body does not have Peng ching, then there is a defect, and if there is a defect, then the body will be blocked and not free-wielding. So, the advice of the boxing classics is to practice each single movement to learn T'ai Chi boxing. You should have the goal of becoming a specialist in each part of the body, and this will not occur suddenly.

Part Four: The Practice of Ch'i Kung

The Wang chronicle says: The Ch'i moves in the blood vessels and tendons, and strength comes out of the skin and bones. In other words, the strength which shows on the outside is the result of the form and the Ch'i which is hidden inside the body. This is the actual phenomenon.

Study the way the body breathes. If you want the breath to flow smoothly and easily, then the breathing should be long and precise. If your breathing is heavy, then your wind becomes rough and short and the flow of Ch'i is disrupted. In addition, never allow the stomach muscles to become tight, as this will prevent the movement of the Ch'i.

In the practice of Ch'i Kung, the first point is to be loose and relaxed and not permit even the slightest exertion which would reduce the velocity of the Ch'i. If you use exertion, then when you encounter someone's energy you will be impeded. Secondly, you must use your concentration to slow down the involuntary muscles and organs. This method is based on the idea of the whole body being empty so that the Ch'i flowing in the blood can move quickly or slowly. The stomach must be relaxed and empty, then the Ch'i can leap and fly. The purpose of these two points is to make the whole body's pipeline of Ch'i active and full of life so no movement will be impeded. Even when this pipeline for the Ch'i has been opened, the Ch'i must still be pushed through it. The pipeline must not be too large, or the pressure of the Ch'i will not be great enough. The real power, however, is not of the Ch'i but of the mind. This is the third main point. Your concentration on the spirit of vitality must be steady and not interrupted. If you are not focused on one point, then the Ch'i will begin to move but eventually become impeded. In T'ai Chi boxing the mind must move the Ch'i. It must command calmness and sinking, then the Ch'i can penetrate into the bones. The mind is the commander and the Ch'i is the messenger. The mind must first give a strict order and afterwards the message can be transmitted. You must force the Ch'i through the pipeline if it is stuck and ensure it flows smoothly. To move it into the bone marrow is very difficult. If the Ch'i can sink then you can be concentrated.

Using these three points regarding the practice of Ch'i Kung, you must receive the spirit and Ch'i into the bones. The spirit is gathered inside so it will not be lost. In movement, ask for the achievement of stillness. From this practice you get the form and style of drawing silk—Peng ching's opening and closing—and then you have inner energy and can say that you have T'ai Chi boxing's form and energy separation. Now take another step. Use mental power and don't scatter the force of the Ch'i. If it is scattered then the body will not contain collecting, and it becomes easy for the Ch'i to be impeded. The spirit of vitality must be made to rise up, and the entire body must be relaxed. The tendons are straight and the Ch'i is lively. The Ch'i is moved calmly and made to penetrate into the spine.

The breathing is smooth and light. The whole body contains the idea of emptiness. To inhale is to close, to roll, to collect. To exhale is to open, to release, to strike. When inhaling, the spirit of vitality is naturally raised. Hidden in this is the idea of withdrawal and attack. When exhaling, the spirit of vitality naturally sinks downward and contains the idea of releasing out toward the opponent. When the mind moves the Ch'i, this is expressed by receiving the Ch'i into the bones. Also it contains the use of calmness and sinking. In the practice of Ch'i Kung, when there is movement there is also contained in it, stillness and calmness. This is essential to the movement. The spirit directs the movement of the Ch'i, but the focus of attention must not be on the Ch'i. If it is then the Ch'i will be impeded. If the focus of attention is on the spirit, then the Ch'i will be lively.

The practice of Ch'i Kung is also about utilizing the four characters of rolling, releasing, collecting, and striking. At this point attention should be paid to rolling and releasing. The rolling and releasing should be calm and cool because in it is the opening and closing. In the function of sinking the spirit of vitality gives the order to the Ch'i to circulate through the line of opening and closing. Closing, then, is from the fingers down to the feet, and opening is from the feet rising up to the fingers along this intersecting line. Then the Ch'i Kung moves from nothing to something, and from something to being lively, and from being lively to strength. You can test the strength or weakness of the Ch'i from the sinking. There is no movement in T'ai Chi boxing which does not have rolling and releasing. The student should pursue this study in order to advance his skill. Relevant examples are numerous, including the following:

1. In Draw the bow shoot the tiger, the upper part is collecting and striking. Are the strikes smooth and sunken?

2. In Deflect downward, parry, and punch, does the movement use central collecting and striking? Does the right side have this sinking?

3. In Downward punch is the strike lower collecting and striking? Does it turn and sink when it strikes?

If you understand the above then you have the achievement of receiving into the bones. This is the function of sinking. To understand this part the preceding three parts must be mastered, because if the drawing of silk is not threaded together, and if the energies are not clearly separated, then the collecting and striking cannot be proper. The will power will not follow the many movements. The rolling, collecting, releasing, and striking discussed here must have strength added to flexibility like drawing a bow, and then the flexibility can shoot out like releasing an arrow. Then the Ch'i Kung can be said to have increased and the meaning is comprehended.

Part Five: The Practice of the Spirit of Vitality

In the practice of the spirit of vitality, the spirit and Ch'i must be roused and the whole body must be without defect. In stillness there must be the energy of movement. It is the mind which moves the spirit and makes the spirit and Ch'i combine, because the Ch'i moves slowly when moved by the mind even though the intention is quick. The intention is the main mover.

The above concept is an example of learning energy separation. It is learning that to get the whole concept one must have the skill of Peng ching. When the whole concept of Peng ching is understood, then Peng ching can be clearly divided into the eight gates without confusion. If you use Peng ching's movement to its downward and inside direction, then it becomes Lu. If you use Lu to its conclusion then you express fully the idea of Lu. If this reasoning is used to express the energy of the eight gates, then the energies can be isolated.

When the idea moves, the spirit follows. The spirit moves and the Ch'i strikes. When the skill of spirit/Ch'i is understood, then there is advancement. Although on the outside the circular movement can be seen, the energies on the inside cannot be perceived because they originate with the will.

The special focus of the spirit of vitality's circular form is to support the square. Striking is the square. To have both the square and the circle is the rule. The square is the foundation and the circle is the use. The movement is circular on the outside and square on the inside. When there is movement, there can be a square within the circle and the point of the rectangle can be used. When outward and inward are used it is called adhering. If there is only circular movement without the square during movement, then you can't revolve. How can you adhere to an opponent and not have the skill of pulling? The Wang chronicle says: T'ai Chi is circular regardless of the kind of movement; don't leave the circular. T'ai Chi is square regardless of the kind of movement; don't leave the square. The square is out and in. The circle is enter and retreat. Follow the square and follow the circle for any direction. When the energy circulates, its center of gravity is expressed as a square. But this square is the blending of the circle and the square, and inside there is the corner of the square. You only feel the circular—not the square—when energy separation is expressed, and the square's corner exists inside and is the synthesis of the idea shooting out and the Ch'i following.

Vitality and spirit are born by the angles of clear energy separation. By the mind's order the smooth and powerful vitality and spirit are raised. It requires extensive practice to get the spirit and the energy to unite. The main point of the spirit is for the energy to be angular. After the spirit and energy are combined, the circle and square are used together yet separated. At this point the body will follow the intention.

The more the spirit is practiced, the more smooth and powerful it becomes. Eventually the body will follow the intention in every movement. But to reach this stage the postures must be accurate and proper. The top of the head must be empty and suspended, because when the top of the head is suspended, then the vitality and spirit can eject strength and focus it on one point. It is not easy to be scattered when the head is suspended from above. If the top of the head is not suspended, then the vitality and spirit will have their strength exhausted; like the attempt to grab a fish, the form will be stupid and miss. This is all collected inside until the time to strike is just right.

When striking, the spirit moves and the Ch'i goes out, and when the Ch'i goes out the energy strikes. When the energy strikes, the spirit, Ch'i, and energy combine. This effect is from the foundation of Connecting and Receiving, and the intention moving the spirit and Ch'i is internal. To execute an order, the spirit and Ch'i must boil. When the spirit and Ch'i boil, the Ch'i moves internally and gradually while the spirit moves outwardly and swiftly. If you want the Ch'i to follow the movement of the spirit, you must practice the Ch'i returning to spirit and make them combine. The spirit arrives and the Ch'i follows. Then the whole body is agile and brisk, lively and alert. It is harmonious and filled with a great power. The lightness and dexterity create a feeling that others will not know. This happens because Peng ching is abundant and the whole body is full and undulating.

In all movements the spirit and Ch'i are stored inside and not revealed outside at all. One can say that it is only will power which is involved. When the set is practiced, make the vitality and spirit inside move and circulate. The key point here is the energy of the empty and suspended top of the head. Make the spirit thread itself to the top of the head and you will be light, you will have dexterity, and then you can prove that in no place in the body is there a defect or shortcoming. There is no place in the body which is not full.

If the body has a defect, it is because one area does not have enough Peng ching. If the body has this kind of shortcoming in its upper part, the problem is at the shoulders. If the shortcoming is in the lower part, the problem is at the thigh and hips. If the shoulders rise up, then the hand and the body are two separate parts. If the thigh or hip is twisted, then the thigh and the body are two separate parts. Then the whole body is three separate parts. The body must be one single unit and not separate parts. Pay special attention to the shoulders and the hips to ensure that they don't rise up. The entire body should be a smooth and gradually curved line, and every joint should correspond with the other joints to the proper degree. This is the phenomenon of the body without short-comings. If there is an external defect, it is easy to correct. But, if the defect is internal then it is not so easy to discover. If the inside has a defect and the outside has no defect, it is still a defect and the whole body does not have the concept of one unit without sep-arate parts.

The boiling of the spirit and Ch'i can be tested through the skilled use of the square and circle. The foundation of the square and the circle is that the energies are clearly isolated. So, to under-stand the vitality, spirit, and Ch'i Kung, the first three parts of this chapter must be learned. Ch'i Kung's main point is that it can be concealed, and the spirit of vitality's main point is that it can be manifest. Concealing is receiving and sinking. Manifesting is the boiling of lightness and dexterity. The practice of the spirit of vital-ity is that in stillness there is action or movement, and lightness and dexterity are critical. In Ch'i Kung practice, in movement there is stillness, and sinking is the key point. When the spirit and the Ch'i are made to boil, then you can suddenly conceal or suddenly manifest. In practicing the set, lightness and sinking are divided to prove that there is no defect and that the spirit is outwardly man-ifested.

Part Six: Uniting the Inside with the Outside

In this practice the inside and the outside must be united. The entire body is one connected unit. In the practice of T'ai Chi boxing, this is an essential without which mastery is impossible. On the out-side are the body, waist, and top of the head. Inside are the vital-ity, Ch'i, spirit, and energy. All movements must follow this rule of union in order to make the body correct and free-wielding.

The body appears relaxed but is not relaxed. It seems to open but doesn't open. It has motion but the motion can't be under-stood. It seems to stop but it never stops. This is because the whole body is completely strung together and connected in every place.

The entire body has a Ch'i which is rising and flourishing. All exchanges have a smooth and easy energy. The boxing chronicles say: In all movements the body is light, agile, and strung together. The spirit and the Ch'i boil and penetrate inside without a shortcoming. Don't be convex or concave. Don't be intermittent. Pay greater attention to the drawing of silk energy than to the striking energy.

The root is at the base, the striking comes from the thighs, and the main power is from the waist then expressed in the fingers. From feet to thigh to waist is one complete movement. The opportunity and the position are determined by the fact that if the energy comes from the front, you retreat backwards. All movements have their origin and intention from the inside, not the outside. When there is an up, there is a down; when there is a front, there is a back; when there is a left, there is a right. If the intent is to move upward, you must start from below. If the intent is to go left, you must start from the right. Empty and solid must be clearly defined. Every motion has this empty and solid. This is what causes the whole body to be strung together. The upper and lower are united. This is the application of movement without interruption.

This section could be called "when one part moves, everything moves." When you are still, then the entire body is still. Motion then is the motion of the inside and the outside together. Opening and closing are governed by principles. Outward and inward are governed by order. Quickness and slowness are born together. Collecting and striking can be concealed or manifest, light or heavy. In opening the Ch'i comes from the bottom to the top, and in closing the Ch'i goes from the top to the bottom. Gradually all movement will follow the intention. When this stage of development has been reached, you then have lively movement.

At this point one does not need to be concerned about the body because the body now follows the intention of the mind. At this point successful habits have been developed. You feel only the mind, not the body. In T'ai Chi boxing, knowledge is forged from the source. The Yang chronicle says that it is a virtue for the body to move when upright. Use the idea of lively power like the wheel. Yin and Yang complement each other without hindrance. The body must be a scale, and the mind and Ch'i rule while the bones and flesh are the servants. This sixth part is a graduation. The following are some simple points to sum up this great idea:

1. When you study the set, energy should be moved in every direction. Movement is smooth and easy and unbroken.

2. When you study drawing of silk, the path from the foot to the fingers is smooth, easy, and continuous.

3. When you study energy separation, the attention is focused on one point at a time. The breathing is smooth and strung together with the Ch'i.

4. When you practice Ch'i Kung, make the line of the Ch'i smooth. Increase the hardness of this line. When you practice the spirit of vitality, make the spirit of vitality manage the Ch'i. This is for lively changes. It is soft, light, and agile in use.

5. When practicing the union of the inside and outside, combine the above four points. The vitality, Ch'i, and the spirit are combined as one, and this is commanded by the mind. If the above is attained, then this is the whole body as one unit.

Part Seven: Getting the Opportunity and the Position

The previous section stated that the entire body acts as one unit. This is the foundation, and when understood, you are prepared to push hands. Push hands requires two people to participate. The only way to evaluate another's energy is through Push hands. From the practice of Push hands comes the understanding of awareness energy.

In the movements, don't overextend or lean back. Follow the curved and attain the ability of Adhere, Stick, Connect, and Follow.

When you practice these four, do not permit the defect of leaning, resisting, or trying to get rid of the opponent, or the body will not behave as one unit. So, from Push hands you get the essence of the body. Don't permit any leaning or inclining. In other words, you must stand like a scale. In order to get the essence of energy separation, don't be intermittent or allow any impediment. The body should be lively like the wheel.

To get the opportunity, keep the body energy separation proper and clear. Then later you can search for the point of the force. Seek out the vacant space or gap between the opponent and yourself. A person's root is below. If you intend to break this root, you must get it to rise up. It is not easy to understand the force of this gap. You get the force by Adhering and Sticking, and the force is aided by Rolling and Releasing. If you don't get the position, the strike will have no effect.

So, practice Push hands. The body is united as a whole. Adhere, Stick, Connect, and Follow are the essential points of Push hands. In order to become skilled at Push hands, the five steps—left, right, enter, retreat, and center—must be mastered. The four primary energies are used inside the circle. This energy must be supported by the four secondary energies (corner hands). Then you have the eight gates and the five steps of Push hands. Nowadays the fashion is the fixed-step method of Push hands using only the four primary energies without foot movement. This was developed by Mr. Ch'en Ch'ang Hsing as a specialized skill and thus modified popular T'ai Chi boxing. This originally had hard and straight energy changing to soft. Gradually this type of Push hands became fashionable. If you research the original Push hands, you will see that it is based on moving steps while pushing hands. When moved outside the circle, the four supporting energies must be utilized and this is called Ta Lu, the great pulling. The fixed-step method using only the primary energies is called Hsiao Lu, the small pulling. Study these categories of Push hands; each one has mysterious uses. Study the fixed-step method first, the small pulling. When first beginning to Push hands, it must be done very slowly in order to have the opportunity to investigate the movements of the hands and body. If this is researched and studied, gradually you can feel inside whether you have the opportunity and the position. Some thoughts to keep in mind:

1. During Chi, which is reversing Peng's energy, is there the defect of leaning or inclining? Is it outward drawing of silk?

2. During Lu, which is Peng drawn inside, is there the defect of inclining? Is it inward drawing of silk?

3. During Peng, is there any leaning? Does the energy move?

4. During An, which is Peng's energy drawn down, is there any leaning? Do you adhere?

5. During Push hands, is the degree of Peng great enough? Is there the defect of stiffness?

6. During Push hands, is the use of Peng excessive? Does the top of the head have any defect?

7. During Push hands, are the retreating steps too large? Do you try to get rid of the opponent?

8. During Push hands, are the advancing steps too large? Is there the defect of resisting?

If Adhere, Stick, Connect, and Follow are comprehended with no defects, then you have successfully completed the first step of Push hands.

Part Eight: Sacrificing Yourself to Follow the Opponent

The preceding part addressed the opportunity and the position. To sacrifice yourself to follow the opponent is the initiative, and the opportunity and the position are the passive. When the opponent's hard energy comes, you must turn. Don't try to get rid of his energy by stepping back or pushing away. If you intend to close without moving, use K'ung, Chieh, Tso, and Jou or you will not get the use of turning without stepping back.

K'ung (empty)

This force causes the opponent to overextend and drain his energy. It is done in any direction. The opponent is not permitted to get away. While you drain the opponent's energy, you drain your own at the same time. If a person's Peng ching is overextended greatly, you must avoid being moved outside the circle and you must adjust this energy. This is the method of draining your own energy and the opponent's energy. This is K'ung ching, the method of draining energy.

Chieh (binding)

This causes the opponent's Peng ching to be insufficient. You feel the position of the opponent's energy. Your own Ch'i increases Peng ching inside, and the opponent is not able to express or execute his energy. If the degree of your own Peng ching is weak, you cannot effectively adhere and stick. You must thread the Ch'i. This is the method of supporting the opponent's energy, and repairing your position and thus repairing the Ch'i. The position cannot be repaired with force. If force is used, it is a defect. Regardless of whether Chieh is of yourself or your opponent, it is the method of connecting the Ch'i.

Tso (break)

This causes pressure not emptiness so energy can be delivered. The energy must sink down and afterwards fall. To change this energy, you must change the inside energy of drawing silk. If Tso is taken to its extreme, it becomes folding. This is the inside use of draining. It is internal pulling energy, which pulls the opponent's foundation.

Jou (weak)

This causes the opponent's energy to become weak. If your position is not repaired enough or slightly off balance, the body exchanges its own energy. It moves towards the outside and up. It is outside drawing of silk. If Jou is taken to its extreme, it become releasing. This effect is utilized from the inside, adding in the outside to pull the opponent's root.

Generally K'ung, Chieh, Tso, and Jou are used after the opponent moves and depend on the circumstances. It can said that their use is completely passive. If you can follow your opponent then it is easy to be lively. When you can sacrifice yourself to follow the opponent, then you can feel whether his energy is great or small, light or heavy. When this feeling occurs, it causes you to move and afterwards Adhere, Stick, Connect, and Follow.

Follow the square and assume the circle. Follow the bent but assume the straight. Then you can manage to separate the direction of the opponent's energy and have a clear idea of his intentions—how he comes and goes, the long and short of how he moves. If you are not skilled in following opponents, then you must use force. If you can follow and see every intention, then your ideas will be lively. When you follow, make judgments and measure the enemy like a scale to know if the movements are large or small. Then you can develop the skill of intuiting others' energy. If you just blindly follow the opponent, there is no way to attack.

Without a method you can't protect yourself from harm. So, following the opponent has rules. You must receive, extend, and continue his energy. Slightly change your body and again follow. This is the method of receiving energy. Otherwise you will sacrifice yourself to profit the opponent.

It is difficult to follow men. Your own body must have the opportunity and position, so when following the opponent, he will feel that he does not have power. You get the opportunity from the gap between the bodies. It is from following men that successful collecting and striking occur. So, to follow is to attack. But following and attack are still two different things. At the moment of receiving, the opportunity is rapidly taken.

Examples:

    1. When pushing hands and sacrificing yourself, is your receiving energy excellent?

2. In the evading movements of sacrificing yourself,
   do you get the force? Is there any defect of leaning
   forwards or backwards?

3. When you follow and adhere, do you get the force?
   Is there the defect of being intermittent?

If you can do these things, then you can successfully sacrifice yourself to follow the opponent.

Part Nine: Knowing Yourself and Knowing the Enemy

Knowing yourself is knowing how to move. Knowing the enemy is feeling his movement. You need discipline to have a solid foundation. In all movements be aware of the position of your own energy in order to move the Ch'i. If you intend to know your enemy, first know yourself. The mind moves the Ch'i and the Ch'i moves the body. First use your body to follow the intention of the changes. Then use any of the opponent's changes and know the enemy.

Inside you have K'ung, Chieh, Tso, and Jou to economize. On the outside is the grasping and turning force to consistently use adhere and stick in both directions. If you can adhere and stick, then you can receive and release. If you receive and release repeatedly, stop and use listening energy.

At this point, based on the opponent's changes, collecting and striking must be used in the proper degree only after a reaction. But as this reaction occurs, stop and listen to avoid the opponent's strike without the defect of resisting. Then you can strike him. When practicing T'ai Chi boxing, all movements have this listening energy. The listening must be clear. As soon as contact is made, listen. If you cannot listen then there is no application. If the opponent moves, then borrow this force to follow, collect, and strike. What T'ai Chi boxing calls listening energy is striking energy's first sound. Then you can strike with the body upright and strike from the spine. If the opponent gets the opportunity to slip away, then listen for the use of striking energy. From this listening energy the opponent is made to fall. Four ounces can topple a thousand pounds.

If you can't know the enemy, you can't use this system. If you can't know yourself, you can't move correctly and will not know your own energies. How do you pull the opponent into your circle and make his attempt fail? If you don't know your enemy, how can you make four ounces topple a thousand pounds? This is difficult. Awareness energy knows the enemy first by your bearing, and the energy separation must be correct in every way. When the enemy's energy comes, your energy responds. When the enemy's energy moves in the least bit, it is an opportunity to take advantage of this force. You take advantage of the vacant space, the gap between bodies. When the enemy moves, he will drop! If the enemy does not move, you don't move. If the enemy moves just the slightest bit, you move first. Borrow the energy to strike the man. At that point, getting the position is the primary consideration. If you don't get the position, the result is being double-weighted without change. At the first sign of action, the measurement is internal like the circle of the Yin and Yang. This is called knowing yourself and knowing the enemy. After this is really grasped, one hundred wars, one hundred victories.

The preceding nine sections are the essence of all the boxing chronicles. The principles are compiled here. They teach the correct course of action. The fourth to the seventh sections are meant to perfect Push hands. If you don't push hands, you can't learn. The Push hands opponent should be at least as skillful as yourself if you want to progress, or defects will occur in the movements.

The above is the basis and principles of "Kung Hsin Chieh." Study and research the three steps of Push hands. Understand its theory and principles. T'ai Chi boxing theory says: "Divide clearly the energy of the eight gates and use the five steps." It is the essence of the Wang chronicle. The Huang chronicle organizes it. The order of learning came from the Li chronicles. This is the science of the spirit of vitality clearly illustrated. This knowledge must be examined hundreds of times.

Regardless of what set you practice or what school of T'ai Chi boxing you are from, you must practice according to the principles. If you only practice the T'ai Chi boxing set, the principles will not be understood according to the theories. Push hands must be practiced according to the instruction of the theory. If the set's inner energy is not separated, the five steps are not complete, practice is not done in the correct order, and its meaning will not be understood. Without the guidance of Wang Tsung Yueh, it cannot be called T'ai Chi boxing.

If you don't realize all movements, then the T'ai Chi boxing principles have been missed. How can the light overcome the heavy or the slow overcome the fast? T'ai Chi boxing theory says that if a point is missed at the center, it will miss by a thousand miles at the circumference. Be wise in your progress and avoid regrets. If you insist upon succeeding, why use force to overcome men? So we respond with caution. What is left behind is a standard. Study and research the real meaning of this boxing and you will have double the result with half the effort. The theory left behind in the boxing chronicles will cause you to study and improve and avoid problems. The proper T'ai Chi boxing is contained in "Kung Hsin Chieh." It is about the meaning of the eight gates and the five steps. Study their relationship and answer the question for yourself. The following is a summary of the nine steps of learning T'ai Chi boxing:

1. The Order of Learning T'ai Chi Boxing

Part One: The study of the set and the division of the categories. Use part one for study.

Part Two: The study of drawing of silk. Isolate the movements of the twelve drawings of silk. Use the second part for study.

Part Three: The study of energy separation. Learn Peng, Lu, Chi, An, Tsai, Lieh, Chou, and K'ao. Use the eight gates and five steps to clarify the definition.

Part Four: The practice of Ch'i Kung. Learn to rise and sink while relaxed, and learn to roll, release, collect, and strike. Use the third part for study.

Part Five: The practice of the spirit of vitality. Learn to boil inside with no shortcomings. Use the third part for study.

Part Six: The practice of the inside and the outside being united. The energy of the spirit/Ch'i is strung together. Use the first, second, and third parts for study.

Part Seven: Analyze getting the measurement and the force. Learn adhere, stick, connect, and follow. Rid yourself of the defects of muscle against muscle, being rigid, trying to get rid of the opponent, and resisting. Use the fourth part for study.

Part Eight: Sacrifice yourself to follow the opponent. Learn the grabbing of evading and giving. Learn K'ung, Chieh, Tso, and Jou. Use the fifth part for study.

Part Nine: The question of knowing yourself and knowing the enemy. The sudden reaction. The return strike. Use the sixth part for study.

2. The Foundation of Centrifugal Force

The weak overcomes the strong

[Drawing of silk is revolving]

Form of movement

Inward drawing of silk is closing	Outward drawing of silk is opening
Lu	Peng
An	Chi
K'ung	Chieh
Tso	Jou
Roll	Release
Collect	Strike

The slow overcomes the fast

[Waist and spine are inside the circle]

Chief movement

Drawing the back long is up and down	Relaxing the waist is left and right
Straight Wrist	Bent Knee
Sink Elbow	Butt In
Normal Chest	Head High
Sink Shoulders	Upright Body

3. Lightness and Dexterity are Revolving

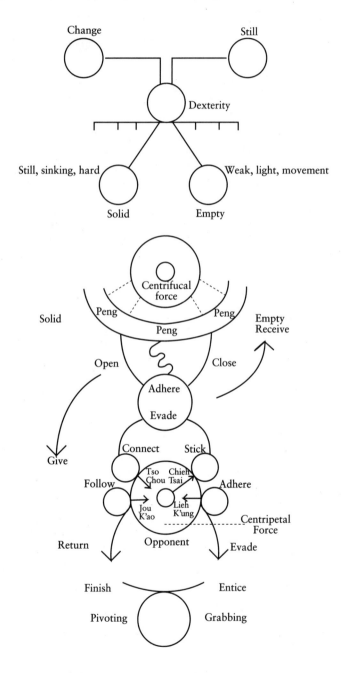

4. The Seventy-Two Essential Terms of the Chinese Boxing Art

Generally, a speciality of any kind has a vocabulary that illustrates how the system is used. The language of this art is paramount to a complete understanding of the subject matter. A word is a symbol of an idea. If the word and the meaning are not specific and clear, it is difficult to understand this art. You must pass through many years of being taught and studying. Then the terms will become certain and fixed. When you learn the language of T'ai Chi boxing, and the meaning of the terms is not clear, then it is not easy to receive the proper vitality from the fixed movements. In order to pass down the mystery of the specific terms, algebra should be used instead of arithmetic. It takes years to get. One can say this is old-fashioned because you cannot escape the fact that the more errors, the more distant the goal. Don't deviate from the boxing art's main theme. Today there is much doubt about the meaning of T'ai Chi boxing's terminology. If the basic terms are not understood eventually, it will be like groping for the meaning in a mist. One needs to be exact and specific in order to proceed. Then an error in the center will not be an error of a thousand miles at the circumference. The terms are explained as follows:

1. Peng ching—The energy of flexibility and resilience. It is the practice of Ch'i Kung strung together inside. It makes the body like a spring or rubber band.

2. Lu ching—The energy of friction and rubbing. It is shifting the direction of Peng ching inside and down, causing the direction of Peng and Lu to be mutually attached or corresponding.

3. Chi ching—This is the energy of two forces combined and changes the direction of Peng. Both hands usually work together and it is a releasing out energy.

4. An ching—Pressing down with the hands and not disconnecting. It is being fixed to a point on the opponent. It is used to cause a reaction by the opponent and does not cause him to fall directly.

5. Tsai ching—The energy of two forces divided. It is grasping a point on the opponent so that he cannot issue forth a strike. It is a method of connecting and stopping the opponent from slipping away.

6. Lieh ching—This is striking energy. During revolving it is collecting great flexibility and then striking out. It is entering the opponent.

7. Chou ching—This is the elbow striking by moving the arms up and down. It is using Lieh's second line of defense.

8. K'ao ching—A strike by the whole body to upset the energy of the opponent's body. It is using Lieh's third line of defense.

9. Adhere energy—This is being fixed to one point on the opponent and not moving from it. It is like taking root on this point. Regardless of what changes occur, you adhere to this point.

10. Stick energy—To be like glue when moving. It is to be fixed to one part of the opponent close and tight. Whatever the movement, you do not move from this surface.

11. Connecting energy—In retreating you have pulling energy. You extend the opponent's energy towards the inside of your circle and grab.

12. Following energy—In entering it has the energy of pushing. It is your energy extending into the opponent's circle and striking.

13. Empty energy—Draining an opponent's energy. When he inclines towards you, it drains his energy and makes him stumble.

14. Bind energy—It is supporting or aiding another's energy. It is using the opponent's stiff energy and supporting it with your own energy. Your energy supports in two directions while tightly attached to his body and allows you to pull.

15. Break energy—Energy which turns towards the inside and down. Its posture wraps inside. It is empty draining energy and prevents the opponent from getting a good position.

16. Rubbing energy—Energy which turns away outside and up. Its posture is outside and away. It is a dissipating energy and prevents the opponent from getting a good position.

17. Tangle energy—A screwing action which circles around the opponent. It revolves around a fixed point and does not let the opponent get away.

18. Receiving energy—Extending your own energy and giving it length. You evenly receive another's energy and continue to lengthen.

19. Stirring energy—Like the joining of the bamboo shoot, the energy is inside. It is continuously receiving the opponent's energy and completely forming this corresponding line.

20. Rousing energy—This is sudden and shocking. The whole body rolls, collects, and afterwards suddenly strikes.

21. Twisting energy—The body turns sideways. It is the turning of the body that changes the energy. It is not hard or stiff and does not resist.

22. Returning energy—The inside spirals or twists and the outside does the returning. It is a grasping energy which does not stop during return or release.

23. Provoking energy—Induces an energy to emerge. It is a revolving pressure which causes a reaction.

24. Grabbing energy—A snatching of the joints using the fingers. The opponent's body is partially caged through bone locking.

25. Exchange energy—This is shifting with partial energy and exchanging the energy of the joints. You greatly open the opponent's joints and change him.

26. Concluding energy—Suddenly releasing and showing energy. This is to catch someone off guard when there is a gap between bodies. Then enter and strike without separating Lieh, Releasing, and Striking.

27. Taking energy—Another gives you his energy. It is the opponent's energy which comes. The rolling and releasing is calm and smooth.

28. Giving energy—The opponent receives your energy. Never be stingy but send it out firmly, sink down, and give.

29. Rolling energy—The large circle changes to the small circle. One uses the spiral from the large to the small circle.

30. Releasing energy—The small circle changes to the large circle. One uses the outward spiral from the small to the large circle.

31. Collecting energy—This is the energy of the bow. It is adding in Peng ching and rolling and releasing so that the bow is ready to fire.

32. Striking energy—Its nature is sudden and straight. It comes from the release of flexibility and strikes out. It can be Lieh or Releasing.

33. The two concepts—They are of equal importance when meeting strength. They are outward and inward drawing of silk's reciprocal use. This is the achievement of meeting strength.

34. Empty-Solid—A deviation of the center of gravity. The center of gravity is stable while the body is active. This deviation of the center of gravity is what allows activity.

35. The scale—The body stands upright without leaning in any direction.

36. Stationary point—With the vertical comes the horizontal station. With the horizontal comes the vertical station.

37. Defect—The Ch'i is not full. Some part of the body is lacking in Peng ching.

38. Yin-Yang—The two are different yet work together. It is releasing, out, striking, opening, hard, meat, use, Ch'i, body, action, and receiving, in, collecting, closing, soft, bone, foundation, reason, mind, and stillness.

39. Listening energy—Waiting for the opponent to express energy. Wait for his slightest movement and move first by following.

40. Opportunity—If there is opportunity you can succeed. It is getting the opportunity to enter the opponent.

41. The Position—The center of gravity is stable. It is not overextending the two feet yet deviating the center of gravity. Then you are smooth and active.

42. Open-Extend—Adding a large movement to the circle. It is expanding the body from the interior.

43. Close-Contract—Adding a small movement to the circle. It is the degree of contracting the body. It is the Ch'i moving the body.

44. Eight trigrams—They are the eight energy separations. It is during movement that the energies have different positions.

45. Five elements—They are the direction of the five steps.

46. Folding—If something is up it must come from below. If you want to move something up it starts from below.

47. Borrowing strength—Adding speed by following an opponent's direction and adding speed by pulling or following.

48. Ch'i Kung—The oxygen in the blood is regulated by adding Ch'i. It is directed by the will power and moves in an orbit.

49. Pulling—Sinking and changing to dragging or pulling. You utilize the energy of sinking down, which measures the strike. Everything is drawn toward the outside.

50. Outward drawing of silk—Revolves toward the outside and up. It is attacking drawing of silk used to force another's energy.

51. Inward drawing of silk—Revolves toward the inside and down. It is defensive drawing of silk and is used to drain another's energy.

52. Bones receive the bamboo shoot—This is getting the point of centrifugal force and then striking the opponent's center of gravity.

53. Movement changes who is in charge—Using centrifugal force, all movements from the waist and spine are focused on a central point. It changes the other's energy.

54. Spirit/Ch'i boil—The spirit and Ch'i are lively and aroused. This occurs during moving energy. The Ch'i follows the spirit, the spirit follows the intention, and all movements are enhanced.

55. Upper and lower united—The hands and feet are divided into empty and solid. It is the relationship of the hands and feet; when the left hand is empty the right foot is solid, and when the left hand is solid the right foot is empty.

56. The whole body is one unit—The entire body is strung together and continuously moves together. When the body moves, no part remains still.

57. Collecting into the bones—The spirit and Ch'i are concealed inside. It is the idea of the tendons lengthening and moving.

58. Awareness energy—Knowing yourself and knowing the enemy. This is to know the opponent's energy and changes and all of his actions.

59. The two shoulders are joined—The two arms are connected by a line between the shoulders. Move one back, the other moves forward.

60. The legs follow each other—The two legs are

connected. This gives them flexibility. When one leg moves, the other must follow.

61. Empty dexterity's top energy—The top of the head has Peng ching. The top is suspended and connected by a line from the top of the head to the middle of the waist.

62. Sinking shoulders, drooping elbows—Don't let the shoulders and elbows rise. Make the elbows sink downward and then the shoulders will sink down also.

63. Contain the chest, pull up the back—Don't make the chest convex or concave. Don't make the chest large. It is the idea of the spine drawn up straight, then the front of the chest is contained.

64. Loosen the waist, open the hips—The waist is like a belt which revolves. It revolves when the body is upright, then the waist can relax.

65. Top defect—The top is overextended in some direction. Then the Peng ching is lacking and you can be bumped or pushed.

66. Stiffness defect—The degree of Peng ching is insufficient. There is no liveliness in more than one direction.

67. Trying to get rid of the opponent defect—This is letting go of the point on the opponent. Losing contact with the opponent will hinder flexibility. The opponent should be close, not far away.

68. The defect of resisting—The response is too distant and too early. Follow the opponent, don't resist.

69. Leaning forward defect—If the front of the body leans forward, this harms the waist energy. It causes the center of gravity to fall forward.

70. Leaning backward defect—When the body leans backward, it causes the chest to protrude. Again, the center of gravity is upset.

71. Breaking off defect—This is breaking off and not remaining in contact with the opponent. It is similar to resisting.

72. Receiving defect—One appears to be receiving but is not. If one receives straight, directly and solidly, it is not using the idea of the wheel.

The above seventy-two definitions are T'ai Chi boxing's most frequently used terms. The definitions are useful for understanding the T'ai Chi boxing system. One must study and contemplate deeply in order to be sure that the correct meaning matches the definition. This will prevent the student from straying from the main road. Progress in this skill is slow, and you must labor ardently to understand the objective of this boxing method. The results one gets from practice are seriously connected with the understanding of the above definitions. Study the source of these terms with diligence and translate their meanings because these are boxing's essentials. The purpose of these terms is to contain them within your body, but without these terms as a standard criterion, the basic points will only be general and not completely clear. Without the terms, your activity appears to be but is not T'ai Chi boxing.

5. The Yin–Yang Summary by C'hen Ch'ang Hsing

Completely Yin without Yang is weak.

Completely Yang without Yin is rigid.

One Yin with nine Yang is a club.

Two Yin with eight Yang is scattered.

Three Yin with seven Yang is stiff.

Four Yin with six Yang is good.

But five Yang with five Yin is called the mysterious hand.

The mysterious hand's one movement.

One T'ai Chi after action completes and returns to nothingness.

The T'ai Chi boxing principles are based on China's unspoiled way of virtue. Confucius and Mencius used it as a battle of the heart. Its concepts were used for oratory skills as a battle of the mouth. Sun Tzu on the Art of War used the ideas to battle populations. And Ch'ang San Feng applied the concepts to the individual's body. Although the tools used for the above four endeavors are different, the principles for use are the same. Regardless of what school you are from or what teacher you have had, whether you have a large or small body, or your form uses large or small circles, inwardly you must use the foundation and essence of the T'ai Chi boxing principles to attain the result of successful progress.

The T'ai Chi boxing chapter "Kung Hsin Chieh" is the standard. It has two uses. One use is self cultivation, and the other use is controlling men. If one practices according to this chronicle, the result can be great success in martial arts. If, however, one is lacking in one area of this skill, then it cannot be said that this is T'ai Chi boxing's illumination.

Because the boxing chronicle's chapters are many and complex, the meaning is not easy to grasp or always clear. If the knowledge is incomplete, then misinterpretation of the movements will be unavoidable and you must strive to understand the practice of the remaining key points. Organize the two concepts. One is practice of the nine principles, and the other is the use of the nine principles for martial arts. Concentrate your efforts on one principle until you are absolutely sure of its correctness. Then practice another category of the principles until it is fully understood. This way you will do half the work with double the result. This way you won't dig a well and not find water.

Chapter Six

Guidelines for T'ai Chi Application

The Nine Principles of the Practice of T'ai Chi Boxing

All T'ai Chi boxing movements have outward and inward drawing of silk. These two represent the in and out lines of revolving. This drawing of silk rises from the legs to the waist and spine and is finally expressed in the hands and fingers. It passes through the nine joints of the body and is always smooth and never sporadic. Striking energy can break off or be intermittent, but drawing of silk never breaks off. In all cases, if there is not a double outward or double inward, or one outward and one inward, then the energy produced will be straight energy. All movements must have outward and inward drawing of silk. If not, it cannot be called T'ai Chi boxing's moving energy.

Although there are two basic drawings of silk, depending on their direction they become ten drawings of silk: large and small outward and inward, inside and outside outward and inward, enter and retreat outward and inward, upper and lower outward and inward, left and right outward and inward.

Boxing chronicles say that moving energy is like drawing silk. The entire body is connected and threaded together without interruption.

2. The source of movement is in the waist and spine. When one part moves, the entire body moves.

The waist moves parallel to your foundation, and the spine moves vertically to your foundation. If in every movement the entire body moves, then the waist and spine must be united. In all T'ai Chi boxing movements to the left or right, the movements must be in increments of forty-five degrees using the waist and spine. If the waist and spine move this way, it is easy to rotate or orbit the outward and inward drawing of silk. Then the joints of the whole body—which are the ankles, knees, hips, waist, spine, shoulders, elbows, wrist, and fist—are joined like a string of nine pearls. The movements are from the back not from the chest or belly, and are threaded together and connected everywhere. If the movement is not from the waist and spine, then the striking energy will not follow through in some part of the body. This cannot be called T'ai Chi boxing's movement.

Boxing chronicles say move the Ch'i like a thread with nine pearls on it without deviation. The waist is the prime mover, the intention gives its order to the waist and spine, and the entire body is strung together without interruption like the nine pearls. The Ch'i sticks to the back while the pulling motion comes and goes.

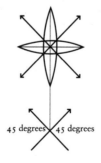

45 degrees   45 degrees

3. Folding transitions are connected without interruption.

Folding is done with the hands, revolving is done with the legs. Folding brings the opponent's movements to the extremity; thus you fold when you receive. It lengthens energy and is never intermittent or broken off.

If you intend to move upward, then first fold from below. If you intend to move to the left, then the folding must start from the right. This way the energies are mutually connected. Also, a firm grasp of this drawing of silk exists, so one never receives straight, directly, or rigidly. This contains the idea of the hands working together in accordance with the steps. Regardless of whether you enter forward or retreat backward, the steps must follow the turning of the body to the left or right. Never enter straight or retreat rigidly. The energy inside the legs is stable and sinks without being intermittent or broken off. Boxing chronicles say that the forward and returning motions must have folding; enter and retreat must have revolving.

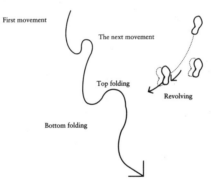

4. The limbs are drawn long to create Peng ching.

T'ai Chi boxing from beginning to end, whether in stillness or movement, must have Peng ching (potential energy). If any part of the body does not have Peng ching, it is a defect. When Peng ching is present then there is flexibility. Without Peng ching there is no flexibility. Flexibility comes from the limbs being drawn up long like a bowstring on a bow.

In T'ai Chi boxing practice, the whole body and its four limbs must follow the rule of being drawn up long. To sink the shoulders and lower the elbows is the drawing up and lengthening of the hands. It is the bowstring of the hands. To contain the chest and draw up the back is empty dexterity's top of the head energy. The top part is drawn up, and the bowstring is the back. The Ch'i sinking to the Tan T'ien is the lower section being drawn up. These three are the drawing up of the whole body and constitute the three body bows which were described already. Tuck in the butt and center it, bend the knees—this is the drawing up of the legs. This drawing up like pulling a bowstring embodies flexibility and is Peng ching. The following are Peng ching's different positions, which are the eight gates:

1. Upwards and to the outside movement is called Peng ching.

2. When Peng is toward the inside it is called Lu ching.

3. When Peng is downward, adhering, and sticking it is called An ching.

4. Both hands with Peng combined inside is called Chi ching.

5. Both hands with Peng divided and toward the back is called Tsai ching.

6. Peng suddenly shoots out is called Lieh ching.

7. The hand forced out of the circle and aided by the elbow striking is called Chou ching.

8. The elbow forced out of the circle and aided by the body striking is called K'ao ching.

The energy of the eight gates is always Peng ching, but the position and use are different. In the practice of T'ai Chi boxing the entire body must be drawn up like a bow, and this is called relaxing. It is T'ai Chi boxing's single most important energy. T'ai Chi boxing's moving energy must use the energy of the eight gates, which is concealed within the body and limbs. If a connection between any joint has a defect, then the joint has no Peng ching. If it is not planned this way, then the inside of the body is just empty with no meaning. If the body does not contain Peng ching and is empty, how can flexibility be tempered one hundred times? How can you call this the eight gates and five steps of T'ai Chi boxing? Boxing chronicles say that moving energy is like tempering steel one hundred times. The body is light, full, and the top of the head is suspended. The softest and later the most hard.

5. The body is upright and can withstand impact from all directions.

If the body is upright it can react to pressure from any direction. This is the utilization of Peng ching. If you lean towards the front, then the back has no Peng ching. If you slant to the left, then the right has no Peng ching. No place in the body should be without Peng ching, and then no place in the body will have a shortcoming.

If you are weak in this area, you will miss the concept of T'ai Chi boxing's circular liveliness. During moving energy the body revolves a great deal and it is difficult to avoid overextending while receiving and releasing. The complete waist down to the tail must be centered and upright. If not, you will miss out on the foundation of flexibility. The whole body equally must collect and strike. Boxing chronicles say: The tail is centered and upright and the spirit is threaded to the top. Make the waist like a flag and there will be no shortcomings.

6. Divide empty and solid. The upper and lower follow each other.

If revolving is done with dexterity and liveliness without impediment, it is due to the division of empty and solid. When first practicing T'ai Chi boxing, you divide into a large empty and a large solid. Later the empty and solid become less and less obvious until finally the difference between empty and solid is clear but very minute. First the empty and solid of the hands and feet are divided about twenty percent to eighty percent, then later about thirty-five to sixty-five percent. Lastly one foot will have fifty-one percent and the other forty-nine percent. Because when the empty is to a greater degree small, then the changes become much faster.

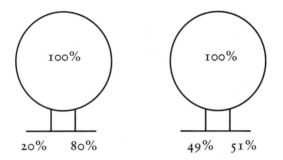

The two hands and feet must have empty and solid clearly divided. After long practice you will have the habit of the hands and feet being balanced with empty and solid. When the hand's upper Peng is empty, the lower part sinks and is solid. If the left hand is empty, then the left foot must be solid. If the right hand is solid, then the right foot must be empty.

In T'ai Chi boxing's every position, the hands change from empty to solid and the feet follow in reverse. This is called the achievement of the upper and lower coordinated. When the upper and lower parts are coordinated, you have control of the energy. You are upright and not leaning. It is a unique practice to this boxing art and not easy to rectify if bad habits are formed. Boxing chronicles say: The entire body must be divided into empty and solid, and the parts must be coordinated. The intention and the Ch'i must have dexterity to gain circular liveliness. So it is said, change from empty to solid.

7. With each step, move like a cat.

Stepping like a cat resembles a cat catching a mouse. The rear foot sticks to the earth and the front foot moves. If the front foot is put down heavily, it has not divided the empty and solid to the proper degree. This will cause your foundation to rise up, and this is not T'ai Chi boxing's foot method. While the steps rotate from empty to solid, the drawing of silk must also be used and you will be able to rotate while the steps are made. Do not enter or receive in a straight way. Be careful that although the upper body is T'ai Chi that the lower body does not have a defect.

8. Collect the nine joints in a curved way. Open the bow and fire.

If you intend to strike, great flexibility must be generated. This energy is curved collecting. In order to collect firmly and strike hard, the nine joints must collect equally. The spine is the leader and the collecting cannot be straight collecting. The body, hands, and feet must collect by the rotating of the drawing of silk. This collecting motion is felt when you receive pressure or force.

Collecting can be done outwardly or inwardly. When the collecting becomes complete or full, then slightly revolve in a direction and from the spine you strike. When striking, the nine joints move equally and strike one point. This way the striking energy is upright and not leaning in any direction. This way of striking is like an arrow piercing a target. The energy is relaxed and neatly beamed to one focus at a time. When striking, one hand is the chief and the other hand is the servant and the two exchange simultaneously. In other words, when striking the two hands must have empty and solid.

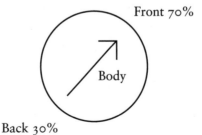

Boxing chronicles say: Energy must be curved collecting and have surplus. In the curved ask for the straight. Collect and then strike. Striking must be sinking and relaxed and beamed to one point. Collecting energy is like drawing a bow; striking energy is like releasing an arrow. Strength strikes from the spine. Receiving is releasing.

9. The spirit and Ch'i boil. The intention moves the Ch'i.

T'ai Chi boxing's moving energy is like a long river flowing without end. Without end means connected to the opponent without disconnecting. Flowing means that it is like waves or breakers hidden in the water but always coming forth. This is the posture of the spirit of vitality boiling. In order to excel, you cannot just be tossed about by the wind and expect to make the Ch'i collect in the bone marrow. Great flexibility must be added like the drawing of a rubber band.

The Ch'i must be threaded in order to generate great flexibility. The spirit of vitality directs the oxygen, which is a physical phenomenon.

During the outward and inward force, the lower part of the body is tempered, and the spirit of vitality is swift to direct. Everywhere in the body the tissues follow the idea or intention, and this is the foundation for lengthening one's life. So, in practice the spirit of vitality must be raised. It is like the revolving of the axle.

Boxing chronicles say: It is the intention which moves the Ch'i. It commands the Ch'i to sink and penetrate into the bones. It is the Ch'i which moves the body and causes it to be smooth and easy. Then you get the full advantage from your intention. Never be convex or concave. Be like the great river flowing without end. The energy is like a river and the Ch'i is the wheel.

T'ai Chi Boxing's Drawing of Silk

Type of drawing of silk	Direction	Movement name
great, small, outward, inward	revolving	Grasp the bird's tail
upper, lower, outward, inward	divided	White stork cools its wings
left right outward, great small inward striking	striking	Deflect, parry, and punch
left inside, right outside, upper outward, lower inward	revolving	Carry tiger to mountain
great, small, outward, inward	opening	Slow palm slanting flying
double outward	left, right	Wave hands like clouds
double inward	kicking	Turn and kick with heel
double inward	open, close	Strike tiger force
double inward revolving back	striking	Chop opponent with fist
upper, lower, outward, inward	opening	Single whip down
double inward revolving down	divided	Finger block up with fist
left, right, outward, inward	revolving	Cross wave of water lily
great, small, outward, inward	divided	Single whip
left, right, outward, inward	releasing	Brush knee and twist step
left, right, outward, inward	receiving	Apparent close up
inside, outside, outward, inward	closing	Fist under elbow
double inward	lower closing	Deflect, parry, and punch
great, small, outward, inward double inward revolving	opening	High pat on horse
double inward	hidden	Downward fist

inside, outside, outward, inward	revolving	Turn and kick
great, small, outward, inward	entering	Part the wild horse's mane
upper, lower, outward, inward	opening	Golden cock stands on one leg
double inward	entering, closing	Step up to form seven stars
upper, lower, outward, inward	revolving	Shoot tiger with bow
great, small, double inward	closing	Raise hand posture
great, small, outward, inward	receiving	Left right raise hand
left, right, outward, inward	closing	Green dragon out of the water
double inward	retreating	Repulse the monkey
outward, inward	upper opening	Fan through the arm
double inward	opening, closing	Divided kick
upper, lower, double inward	rising	Turn the body two feet up
left, right, great outward, small inward	turning	Diagonal single whip
double outward, inward, revolving inward	revolving	Fair lady works at shuttles
upward, downward, outward, inward	intersecting	Diagonal single whip
left, right, outward, inward	divided retreating	Retreat to ride tiger

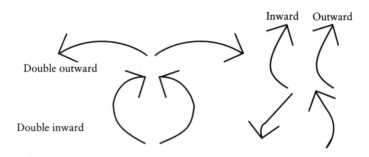

The Nine Rules of T'ai Chi Martial Arts

1. The T'ai Chi armament.

T'ai Chi has striking energy and use. It is the circle of the Yin and Yang. Use is when injury is sustained but the opponent does not fall down. It is Yang. Striking energy is when he falls down but is not injured. It is Yin. Striking energy is the four primary angles (Peng, Lu, Chi, and An). Use is the four corner angles (Tsai, Lieh, Chou, and K'ao). There are two uses for the four corner hands: a) when you defend or ward off the enemy movement, and it is adhering, and b) when the four primary hands are forced out of the circle and this distress must be relieved. Then use the supporting four corner hands. For this you must focus on adding strength in the proper degree. This is not scattered strength like a shotgun. If you don't feel the enemy, you can't strike and then will miss out on the use of martial arts.

2. Add strength to every separate strike.

In T'ai Chi boxing, outside you remove, exhaust, and capture. Inside is the result of practice which allows you to strike out in any direction. Use one hand or two hands and strike out in any and all directions. Once the habits of the target are observed, add strength gradually and then you can engage.

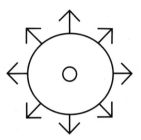

3. Present, Tight, Narrow, and Energy. Open the gate, out goes the hand.

Present	Raising the spirit of vitality so it will not be scattered.
Tight	The posture is closely packed with no gaps.
Narrow	Select the enemy's closest point to your body. Don't reject what is near for what is far away.
Energy	The drawn bow collects energy and waits for the enemy.

These four words are the concept of the gate opens and the hand goes out. If you adhere to the enemy's closest point, there will be no gap for him to take advantage of.

4. Water rubs the shoulders. Enter the circle of the opponent.

The circle is the range or sphere of a man's hands and feet. If you intend to enter the enemy's circle, one hand must attack and one hand must guard. The two hands draw silk, revolve, and enter like water rubbing rocks on the side of a river. One hand turns and rubs, one hand adds water is the basic posture. The body must be completely centered and then enter. You measure the enemy's posture with your shoulders, then you attack and defend, and at the same time defend and attack. This is the most secure method of entering the enemy's circle.

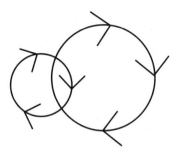

5. Tsai, Lieh, Chou, and K'ao. From the strike, turn and adhere.

Tsai   A system for stopping the enemy's hand and manifesting his energy.

Lieh   Striking the enemy's body and at the same time attracting the enemy's movement.

When Tsai and Lieh are used but your body is forced outside the circle, then Chou will relieve this. If when using Chou you are again forced outside the circle, then you must use K'ao.

6. Adhere, stick, connect, and follow. Gradual and quick respond together.

Adhere and stick are done with the hands. Connect and follow are done with the feet.

Adhere   Sticking to the enemy's one point and not moving from it.

Stick   After you adhere and revolve, first the palm is used to adhere, then it turns and the wrist adheres. Turn and the arms adhere. Thus, sticking is adhering while revolving and not breaking off.

Connect   The enemy's energy comes to attack. Then retreat by revolving the foot but not necessarily stepping backwards.

Follow   After the evading response, step forward and enter and don't leave.

In order to realize these four terms, get rid of the following four defects:

Muscle against muscle	The adhering is overextended and stiff.
Stiffness	The sticking is not enough, you miss when adhering.
Getting rid of the opponent	The following is too curved and you break away.
Resisting	Expanding too quickly and colliding or bumping.

Practice Push hands for a long time and these defects will change into attributes.

7. K'ung, Chieh, Tso, and Jou. The adjustment of adhere and evade.

When you first learn to use energy, the four defects of muscle against muscle, stiffness, getting rid of the opponent, and resisting must be overcome. Then progress to the merits of adhere, stick, connect, and follow. While learning adhere, stick, connect, and follow it is often easy to fall into the habit of leaning forward, leaning backward, breaking off, and receiving straight. These are four more defects. If adhere and stick are not accurate it is usually because the two defects of leaning forward or backward are present. When these two defects exist, and it is time for connect and follow, you can't avoid being broken off and intermittent. So, when you lean forward or backward one area of the body will have a shortcoming and the enemy will gain an advantage. If the defects of breaking off or receiving straight are present, the enemy can take advantage of the gap between your body and his. He will then be able to escape and slip away while adhering and evading. The enemy will not easily be overcome and his energy will not be easy to intuit. So, in order to adhere, stick, connect, and follow, do not break away, do not receive straight without revolving, do not lean forward, and do not lean backward. If any of these defects occur, the adjustment machine (K'ung, Chieh, Tso, and Jou) must be used.

K'ung You revolve at the adhering point and drain energy. Then the defect of leaning forward will be overcome.

Chieh Tightly adhere and add strength which aids or supports the energy. Then the defect of leaning backward will be overcome.

Tso After you bend or revolve to the side, do not retreat. The leg does the revolving but remains fixed. Then the energy will stick, and the defect of breaking off will be overcome.

Jou Using the minutest circle, firmly stick and follow the evading movement. From this point you can strike at any time. The energy cannot be received straight. At this point the adjustment has been achieved.

This will remove the eight above-mentioned defects. Then you have perfected adhere, stick, connect, and follow, which is adhere and evade. It is Yin and Yang working together and is awareness energy.

8. Joining the bones and stirring the bamboo shoot. Directing the strike to a point.

Striking energy must strike the enemy's center of gravity, and then the enemy can be subdued. To strike this point on the enemy, focus on the interior of his center of gravity. To probe this center of gravity is called stirring. You collect, revolve, and strike, and the enemy will be forced to stumble and fall. This is called "joining the bones and stirring the bamboo shoot."

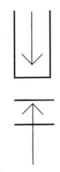

9. The underground spring shoots out.

Striking and releasing use a cutting motion. When you strike and release towards the enemy's point you have received joining the bones and stirring the bamboo shoot. When you strike the enemy's up-and-down line you must form a parabola so the energy can spring out. After you probe the enemy, your heel moves to strike and then the enemy will rise up, his root will be broken, and you can use his energy. The action is like cutting vegetables. One half of the circle drifts back and the other half shoots out and causes the enemy to fail. Then the idea of T'ai Chi is not missed. Also, you can forge ahead without considering the enemy's upper and lower parts because you are concentrated upon his center of gravity.

The T'ai Chi Boxing Book "Kung Hsin Chieh"

1. It is the intention which moves the Ch'i and commands it to sink. Then you can collect into the bones.

[explanation] The intention is the vitality of an idea, which is a general term for will power. In all movements this idea is the prime factor. It orders the Ch'i to move and revolve with every opening and closing. In opening, you must will it to end up at the tips of the appendages. In closing, the intention goes through the back and returns to the Tan T'ien or your center of gravity. In this opening and closing line, the whole body's tendons are stretched out straight (drawn long). This is called relaxing, and then you will naturally contain Peng ching. This Ch'i is connected everywhere and is entered into the bones. During moving energy, if the will power does not appear, the form will appear dull. If the movement is too light or floating, then how can the Ch'i penetrate into the bones?

2. The Ch'i moves the body and commands it to be smooth and easy. Then you will get full advantage from the intention.

[explanation] The Ch'i follows the intention and moves because the intention moves the Ch'i and then the body moves. The Ch'i must be coordinated. In other words, the breathing must be moderate and coordinated. All movements must be elastic whether you rise or fall. You move as a gradual curved line and never allow the defect of being convex or concave. This is called smooth and easy, so the body movements come from the Ch'i and the Ch'i comes from the intention. During moving energy, if the breathing is not coordinated then it is the hand which moves the body, and the energy cannot be generated. Then the body cannot be made smooth and easy, and this is contrary to the advice of the boxing chronicles.

3. The spirit of vitality is raised with no worry of being late. It is called the head being suspended.

[explanation] The two eyes look out parallel to the ground and the top of the head is slightly drawn up; this is empty dexterity's top energy. The vitality and intention are naturally aroused. Also, the top of the head has Peng ching and will lessen the body's weight. Then the revolving motion is naturally light and you won't have to worry about being late or heavy. During moving energy if the top of the head is not suspended this way, the highest point of the body will tend to lean or incline, pulling the entire body. Then the spirit of vitality is not easy to arouse, and being late or heavy will be difficult to avoid.

4. The intention and the Ch'i must revolve with dexterity and have circular liveliness; so it is said, change from empty to solid.

[explanation] In all movements using two hands or two feet, or

one hand or one foot, all of these parts must have one chief and one servant, or one empty and one solid. When empty and solid are present and the Ch'i follows, it is called dexterity. If the intention or focus is on the left, then the left is solid and the right must be empty. If the focus is on the right, then the right is solid and the left is empty. This way the intention interchanges, and the intention and the Ch'i are not impeded at any given point. This is called liveliness. Inside the force is smooth and easy, and the curved line is gradual and moderate; this is called circular. Being smooth and easy is being able to interchange the two hands and two feet or one hand and one foot into empty and solid. This is called changing from empty to solid.

5. The body must be upright and comfortable and able to cope with impact from any direction.

[explanation] The top of the head is suspended and can adjust the balance of the entire body. If the head is not suspended correctly the entire body will incline to the side or lean forward or backward. If the body is centered, all surfaces of the body will have Peng ching. If you lean in any one direction, then impact can be handled from only seven instead of eight directions. During moving energy the Ch'i must sink; then it will not rise up and the body is centered and fixed in one place. The force when applied is a curved line and is gradual. It can revolve easily and the form is comfortable. T'ai Chi movements, regardless of their changes, must have the center of gravity between the thighs and centered through the tail. This is the achievement of the centered upright body. If during moving energy there is frequent leaning or inclining, then the idea of the upright body has been missed. During moving energy, if the body cannot comfortably unfold during the circular movement, the problem is at the top of the head. If impact cannot be handled from any direction, then the hard and soft cannot interact and the rule of the square and the circle will not be understood for its ingenious uses and subtle purposes.

6. When striking you must sink, be relaxed, and beam the focus to one point at a time.

[explanation] Whenever striking energy is intended, the hands and feet must have collecting energy. During striking the body must sink, because sinking makes the opponent's base rise up. When striking do not permit exertion. If exertion is used it is called inactive. If there is no exertion it is called relaxation, and the body is vast and empty and this is called pure. When the tendons inside are straight, and there is the sinking and flexibility, then it is proper striking energy.

During striking energy the two hands are exchanging empty and solid; this way they guard the body's balance. The two hands must have empty and solid clearly divided. In other words, one hand is the chief and one hand is the servant, one hand is light and one is heavy, and this is called focusing on one direction. When you practice T'ai Chi boxing's moving energy and there is no striking energy, there is one defect. When there is striking energy but no sinking, this is a second defect. When there is sinking but empty and solid are not clearly divided, this is a third defect. If these three defects are present, the important striking idea of T'ai Chi has been missed and the concept of martial arts misunderstood.

7. Move the Ch'i like a curved thread with nine pearls without the slightest interruption.

[explanation] Man's body has nine curves. They are the fist joint, the wrist joint, the elbow joint, the shoulder joint, the spine, the waist, the hips, the knee joint, and the ankle joint. Moving the Ch'i through these nine curved pearls means making all movements smooth and easy with circular liveliness like the pearls. It takes advantage of the movement of the Ch'i and means that the body is threaded together everywhere. If during moving energy the nine joints do not all move together, the meaning of "when one part of the body moves, the entire body moves" has been missed. This is one defect. If every joint moves but they are not strung together, then there are two defects. If the movement

is strung together and the Ch'i is moved but you can't take advantage from this movement, then there are three defects. If these three defects are present, it is not possible to collect into the bones.

8. Moving energy is like tempering steel one hundred times. What is firm and flexible will not break.

[explanation] Tempering steel one hundred times makes it pliable. This hardness also has softness. It is not like cotton's softness but is a softness that contains flexibility. So, outside there is softness but inside there is hardness. The inner hardness comes from Peng ching. Peng ching is from the joints being pulled up long, and the inside is strung together with the Ch'i. Like the rubber band, the wheel strikes its C'hi. Because the hardness is tempered one hundred times, the softness is pliable and the inside is firm and grounded. If during moving energy the inside is inactive or stiff without flexibility, then there is one defect. If the whole body is completely soft and the inside has no flexibility, then there are two defects. So, to have flexibility is paramount, like a spring inside of a watch that can absorb shock and keep the machinery working together. This is not soft like cotton; if so, the idea of tempering steel one hundred times has been missed.

9. The form is like a hawk seizing a rabbit. The spirit appears like a cat catching a mouse.

[explanation] Moving energy must appear like a hawk intending to seize a rabbit, hovering and circling and not fixed. It means that the intention is lively and gathered like a cat ready to ambush a mouse. This is about aiding or supporting and about the intention moving the Ch'i, and the Ch'i moving the body. If the form is not like a hawk seizing a rabbit and appears dispirited, and not aroused like a cat following the motions of the mouse, and manifests in a disorganized way, then the practice of T'ai Chi boxing's clear intention has been missed.

10. Quiet like a mountain, movement like a river.

[explanation] Quiet like a mountain expresses the appearance of sinking and not rising. When one part is quiet then all parts of the body are quiet, and this is called "the spirit properly gathered within." Movement appearing like a river is expressed by movement resembling waves which don't stop; they undulate equally like a vast river flowing endlessly. This is called "the Ch'i properly boiling." If during moving energy the spirit is not gathered inside, then the inside parts are not quiet and the Ch'i cannot boil. This is like the water of a pond and not a great river.

11. Collecting energy is like drawing a bow. Striking energy is like releasing an arrow.

[explanation] Collecting energy draws the bow full and gives the bow's back great flexibility. Contain the chest, draw up the back, sink the shoulders, drop the elbows, open the hips, and curve the knees—all these postures move together and recur in a cycle. Striking energy is like releasing an arrow and allows the arrow to enter inside with the idea of piercing the target. T'ai Chi boxing's every force has collecting and striking. From this the body moves correctly. Then the inside movement of the set is proper. If the collecting and striking are not combined, then the strike cannot shoot out. If moving energy collects and the bow does not open, then the strike or the arrow will not release from the spine. This means that the inside of the set does not have collecting and striking and cannot be called a proper set. In the curved ask for the straight. Collect and afterwards strike. Strength strikes from the spine.

12. The steps follow the body's rotation.

[explanation] In the curved ask for the straight. First is the collecting and afterwards the striking is born. It is the collecting which causes the striking to be hard. Every joint has curved collecting before the strike. Collecting also comes from the sinking shoulders, and then the energy can strike out from the spine. This is the energy of the upright body. If the steps follow the turning of the body, then it is achievement. If the body follows the steps, then it is a defect. During moving energy the body moves in a direction and then the steps follow and move. It is the twisting step where the feet do not necessarily move. Without this step, the movements will be out of place. If striking energy is not originated in the spine, then the energy which emerges is not upright. So, if the steps do not follow the turning of the body, and the body follows the steps, this is a great defect and everything is for naught. This cannot be called T'ai Chi boxing's striking energy.

13. Receiving is releasing and releasing is receiving. Break off and return to connect. Connect and return to break off. The returning must have folding. Enter and retreat must have revolving.

[explanation] Receiving is releasing receiving, releasing is receiving releasing. These two are interconnected inside and out, front and back, like the T'ai Chi symbol. It is movement without end. Then strength can be added to Peng ching. If the striking energy must be cut, then the direction of the energy goes outside the body. So, to return and connect is receiving energy. First draw in the energy and then the other's energy can be received.

During receiving energy, never receive straight. It must involve folding in order to get the moving energy to its final point and to change the force. Don't just return but fold and return. So it is said, if the focus is upward it must begin from below. When the folding is present, then receive the energy of the first force and move it downward. This is the method of consistent moving energy. If the enter and retreat are revolving, it is the foot which does the folding, but it is called revolving. So, folding is done with the hands and revolving is done with the legs. The revolving is T'ai Chi boxing's twisting step method. This way enter and retreat are not straight. These two ideas combined are T'ai Chi's meaning.

First the softest and afterwards the most hard. Breathe and have dexterity and liveliness, and the Ch'i is direct and without harm. The energy from the curved collecting has surplus. The intention is the commander, the Ch'i is the messenger. The waist is the flag and the spine is the flagpole. First the body unfolds and afterwards it becomes tight and firmly packed. This is planned in every respect.

Be like a spring for absorbing shock. It is the softest thing but can become the hardest thing. If the breathing is urgent or strained, then the will power is not clear and the intention and the Ch'i will be impeded. If the breathing is deep and long, then the revolving and changes will be calm and possess dexterity and liveliness. The Ch'i moves directly and without restraint when the breathing is natural. Then the body is without harm.

The energy must collect in a curved way and then flexibility arises. If the collecting is overextended and without surplus, then the posture is wooden and the curved collecting is defective. The intention is the chief commander, The Ch'i is the messenger flag which relays the message of the intention. The waist is the great banner flag which stands majestically without leaning. The spine is the flagstaff with a drawn-up back, which makes the spine extended and long.

The first step is to practice a large expanding and a large contracting. The entire body must relax like a bow. The Ch'i arrives at the tips of the hands and the skill progresses. Gradually the expanding and contracting become more proficient, and from the large circle you progress to the small circle. From the circle being outwardly manifest, gradually the circle becomes inwardly concealed and combines receiving and releasing. The rolling then is so minute as to be contained inside.

First is the intention and then the body. The belly or abdomen is relaxed and the Ch'i is collected into the bones. The spirit is comfortable and the body is quiet. Keep in mind that when one part of the body moves, the entire body moves. When one part is quiet, the entire body is quiet. When the pulling motion is made, the Ch'i sticks to the back and is gathered into the bones. During moving energy the intention is the root. The intention moves the Ch'i and the Ch'i moves the body. The entire body is relaxed and the abdomen empty. Everything is from the waist and spine along with the sinking, so the Ch'i can gather into the bones while the spirit is externally quiet and peaceful. The body can focus on one movement without distress, and this is called quiet. This is the method of moving energy. The movement moves equally through the nine joints, and this is the degree of movement. Every joint must have this degree. This accomplishment is the length of all joints being threaded together. They all move at the same time, and they are all quiet at the same time.

The intention is the root of the pulling movement. The Ch'i must stick to the back and move. It is the central part of the back which utilizes centrifugal force. If in every movement the skin on the back never feels firm and taut, then it is only the abdomen which is the central part and the idea is missed. When it is the spine and back which move then the Ch'i can enter into every bone of the body.

14. Inside the spirit is collected, and outside the body is comfortable. Stride like a cat. Moving energy is like drawing silk.

[explanation] When the spirit is gathered internally and is in charge, then it is easy to support the achievement of the inside being hard. When the outside is peaceful, then it's easy to support the outside being soft. "Stride like a cat" means to imitate a cat in ambush beginning to enter. This is not a common step.

Moving energy is like the revolving of drawing silk. This revolving forward and backward is like a screw. When Peng goes out, it is outward drawing of silk. When Lu goes in, it is inward drawing of silk. It works like a screw. If the spirit of vitality cannot be raised up and the inside is not solid, and if the outside is not comfortable, then the spirit of vitality is outwardly scattered and the hard and soft do not work together. If the forward stride is not like a cat catching a mouse, then it is impeded. If the moving energy cannot revolve when drawing silk, then this is straight energy and T'ai Chi boxing's meaning has been missed.

The whole body's focus is on the spirit of vitality, not the Ch'i. If it is on the Ch'i, the movements will be blocked. If the focus is on the spirit of vitality or intention, then the movements will be lively. Ch'i without strength is completely weak, and strength without Ch'i is completely hard. The Ch'i is like the wheel and the waist is the axle. Although the intention moves the Ch'i, the focus is not on the Ch'i or the Ch'i and the strike will be impeded Because the intention or spirit moves quickly and the Ch'i moves slowly.

In order to practice the Ch'i returning to spirit, focus on the spirit is paramount. Then the focus occurs and the spirit moves, and the Ch'i moves to follow. If there is Ch'i without strength, then you are completely soft. If there is strength without Ch'i, then it is completely hard and without flexibility. If the Ch'i is concealed inside then it is soft, and if it is manifested outside then it is hard. When energy goes out, its root is in the Ch'i. If the Ch'i is lively then the energy is lively. If you intend for the energy to be lively, the Ch'i must move everywhere in the body. It is like the revolving of the wheel without pause. In order for the wheel to revolve, it must have a central point to revolve on. T'ai Chi boxing's waist and spine make this axle. So, in all movements it is the waist and spine which are in charge of the axle. If during moving energy the Ch'i cannot be like the wheel and the revolving doesn't move the body and the waist, then the whole body cannot move as a unit. Then, the idea of the slow overcoming the fast has been missed. The above are the uses of T'ai Chi boxing according to the book "Kung Hsin Chieh."

T'ai Chi Boxing's Chart for Evaluating Progress

1. If during moving energy the idea of the spirit of vitality is expressed it constitutes 12 percent of the skill.

2. If the Ch'i can move the whole body and be smooth and easy, it is 10 percent of the skill.

3. If the top energy is empty and suspended without leaning and the movements are light, it is 5 percent of the skill.

4. If the Ch'i has dexterity and liveliness, and the hands and feet are divided into empty and solid while they follow the changes, it is 12 percent of the skill.

5. If the body is upright and the circle and square move, it is 10 percent of the skill.

6. If during striking energy you are relaxed and sinking and have empty and solid divided, it is 6 percent of the skill.

7. If during moving energy the nine joints are expanded and comfortable and strung together, it is 10 percent of the skill.

8. If during moving energy the idea of the inside hard and outside soft is expressed and there is flexibility without rigidity, it is 4 percent of the skill.

9. If during moving energy the form has the idea of the cat catching the mouse and the hawk seizing the rabbit, it is 3 percent of the skill.

10. If during moving energy the movement boils, and when quiet is then gathered inside, it is 5 percent of the skill.

11. If collecting and striking are proper and express the appropriate posture, it is 4 percent of the skill.

12. If every forward and backward movement has folding and the energy is connected, and enter and retreat are in every case revolving, it is 4 percent of the skill.

13. If the striking energy is from the spine and the steps follow the turning of the body, it is 3 percent of the skill.

14. If the forward stride is like a cat catching a mouse and every movement draws silk outward and inward and revolves, it is 12 percent of the skill.

The above fourteen categories are the research and study of the rules corresponding to the book "Kung Hsin Chieh." In order to practice according to the rules, master just one category and then move to another until the practice contains one hundred percent

of T'ai Chi boxing's skill. If there is a shortcoming then subtract
the percentage. This way the degree of progress is certain and not
vague, and the result will be achievement. It is very difficult work
to express one hundred percent in practice. T'ai Chi boxing's "Kung
Hsin Chieh" is the standard and measurement for effective practice. Regardless of what school one learns from, the same rules,
standards, and principles apply.

The Question of the Hard and Soft

We already know that T'ai Chi boxing makes a strong body and
is for self-cultivation. Learning takes time, so follow one teacher,
adopt one style, and learn it from beginning to end to maturity,
and the learning will be accurate and complete. This way the practice is never broken off and a strong body results. Then progress
to another step and grasp the martial arts, forge the T'ai Chi achievement.

Is the T'ai Chi method soft and without strength? Can the internal energy come out this way? From ancient times it has been asked
whether T'ai Chi boxing has only this soft practice method, or are
the teachers generally unwilling to teach the secrets? This book is
the study and research of these questions. Don't hesitate to raise
questions for all to discuss. From the beginning to the end, one
question continues to come up. Is the T'ai Chi boxing method completely soft? Or is it hard and soft?

According to Wang Ch'iao Yu, the famous teacher, there were
two branches of T'ai Chi boxing. One was called Kuang P'ing and
the other was called Pei Ching. Both are from the teachings of Yang
Pan Hou. The Kuang P'ing school's most famous descendent was
Ch'en Hsiu Feng. Ch'en Hsiu Feng served Pan Hou in the city of
Pei Ching. He observed the Pei Ching school and the Kuang P'ing
school. They are not in the least alike. He confidentially asked Pan
Hou to differentiate between the schools. Kuang P'ing school has
hard and soft. Is the Pei Ching school completely soft?

Yang Pan Hou first smiled and said, "Among the Pei Ching

school there are many honorable men, but they practice boxing out of curiosity and play. Compared to the Manchu the nature and constitution of the body are different. The Manchu is not a Han. Do you understand?" Ch'en Hsiu Feng gave his deepest regards for this talk and he didn't dare ask again. In those days the Manchus ruled China. They oppressed and killed and took everything to its most bitter extreme. All were men of China. Who could not bear a grudge in the heart? But there were those clear-headed men who knew how to make use of the Manchus. In those days the Yang family was employed in the service of the Ch'ing dynasty. They managed the practice and teaching of the war arts for the Manchus. Who could believe that the Yang family should teach compatriots to kill each other? But Pan Hou did not teach them everything— only enough to learn T'ai Chi boxing's form. He did not teach them the T'ai Chi boxing method or achievement. He taught them to be soft as cotton but not how to acquire the astounding skill, so that they would not kill each other. He put them in a passive mode and compelled the royal families to get absorbed in mysticism so they would endlessly pursue a mental achievement.

In those days the Yang family did teach some villagers the Kuang P'ing style. Then during training they used the hard and soft method at the same time. Pan Hou trained their strength properly in accordance with T'ai Chi boxing's "Kung Hsin Chieh," which says: Extreme softness and afterwards extreme hardness. First expand and then contract. This answered Ch'en Hsiu Feng's uncertainty. This helped him to search out the meaning. The Yang family said, "In Pei Ching there are many honorable men but they practice boxing out of curiosity and play. You can see that the royal families have bodies like golden cups and jade leaves. They have not tasted hardship. They practice with the intention of showing off their fashionable inner strength and that is all." Pan Hou also said: "Manchus are not Han, do you understand? The distinction between these men is very clear. One type of man learned the difficult way, properly. Can you distinguish?" So, the Pei Ching school is completely soft, and the Kuang P'ing school has hard and soft. The

practice methods are different. We can believe and rely on Yang
Pan Hou's explanations to Ch'en Hsiu Feng. The advice of Pei
Ching's Wang Ch'iao Yu and Yang Pan Hou is recorded, because
they were masters. Let them explain T'ai Chi boxing from their
records. If you don't receive the real teaching of T'ai Chi boxing,
then you can only get a strong body. You can practice boxing for
ten or more years and in the end only be confused. You can assume
that the real teaching is hard to get. If you practice in accordance
with ordinary methods, you will cultivate a strong body, which is
more than enough, but if you want to succeed in the real power
of T'ai Chi and become perfect, then you must receive the real
teaching. You must define this mysterious method; otherwise you
will practice for years and in the end still be confused, because you
couldn't practice out the real skill. Master Wang, honest and sincere, talked about the method. To understand the real skill, your
heart must look into a clear mirror. That way, in addition to T'ai
Chi boxing's soft outer form you can completely understand the
method. Now we will continue to discuss how to practice.

We already introduced Yang Pan Hou. Pan Hou and his brother
Yang Chien Hou followed their father Yang Lu Chan and his boxing practice from early childhood. It was toilsome and difficult and
they wanted to escape. They were tired and discouraged and thought
about becoming Buddhist monks. The two of them just could not
stand the pain and suffering of practice. In those days to practice
was to endure hardship and to be determined. It was not just a soft
boxing style.

Regarding the question of the hard and soft, Master Wang
Ch'iao Yu once gave an explanation: "If you only desire to cultivate a healthy body then do a soft practice. It will give vitality and
benefit the body and mind. If you want martial arts, on one hand
you must know how to be soft to neutralize the enemy, and on the
other hand you must know how to be hard to attack the enemy."
Hard and soft must be combined to attain this function. If you
want to attain this skill, then you must do a bitter practice, and receive instruction from a qualified teacher. My teacher Wang Ch'iao

Yu, and his teacher Yang Pan Hou, taught boxing in a way which was at first very bitter. But in the present day it is different. It is made easy. Ordinary men just can't stand the old way of learning. You must practice boxing like you want to succeed in getting the real skill and create a perfect body. If you only rely on the soft and don't use strength, like duckweed floating on water, the practice method is not going to succeed.

T'ai Chi boxing's road to success is to be able to distinguish between the Form, the Method, and the Achievement. What is T'ai Chi boxing's successful way of attaining the real power and proper skill? What is the practice procedure? These are problems for the reader to resolve. To address these questions we will divide the discussion into two parts:

1. The hard neutralizes the soft.

First to have then not to have. This is why it is best to first enter the gates of Shao Lin. Then you already have Shao Lin's strength. Your base is stable and the body's vitality is brimming with energy. Afterwards, enter the gate of T'ai Chi. From the beginning Ch'ang San Feng, Yang Lu Chan, Ch'ang Sung Hsi, Chieh Feng Chih, and other great masters first came this way. They all had refined and peerless Shao Lin as a foundation and then shifted to T'ai Chi. They ascended the boundary of spiritual change. In those days C'hang San Feng formed T'ai Chi boxing and said, "First Shao Lin's method and then change." He created T'ai Chi's slow form along with Shao Lin's hard and soft method. The fast and slow changing power is the achievement. So, he only needed to depend on T'ai Chi boxing's form and Shao Lin's method.

Remember what Master Wang said, and what Mr. Pan Hou, and Tung Hai Chuan of Pa Kua, and Kuo Yun Sheng of Hsing I said. They researched and studied the method. The hand goes out hard and solid, quick as lightning. This is the result of the T'ai Chi boxing style. A complete man in two ways. Everyone is surprised. Consider that Mr. Pan Hou's strikes are really Shao Lin and not T'ai Chi boxing. This is because people do not understand T'ai Chi boxing's real mystery. You must know T'ai Chi boxing's slowness is Shao Lin's method also. It is not just lightly blown by the wind like duckweed on water. When T'ai Chi boxing is applied to guarding against an enemy and you only use its slow form, not its hard and swift method, then you will take a beating. So, regarding T'ai Chi boxing's Form, Method, and Achievement, these must be clearly distinguished by the student. Then you can say you are approaching the entrance to the path of the advanced stage of learning.

2. The soft changes to hard. First nothing then something.

When you first begin the study of T'ai Chi boxing, you have no strength and later you have strength. First soft and then change to hard. It takes a long time to get this skill. You must toil hundreds of times and then you can understand it. This book is the study of a speciality. It studies the nature and characteristics of the art and keeps no secrets. Don't dare to play the expert, as this eternally prevents students from getting it (solving the reasoning of T'ai Chi boxing). Master Wang Tsung Yueheh made the following revelation public as follows:

The first step:

First study T'ai Chi boxing's form. We usually see T'ai Chi boxing practiced softly, moving here and there with no strength. This is T'ai Chi boxing's form. Students must first follow a teacher and learn the form's thirteen-fist style. When practice is complete you have become accurate. Practice long—very few students get this skill in less than three years. You must practice every day. The meaning of this soft and slow practice is sensitivity. It is only T'ai Chi boxing's first step to enter the gate of skill and that is all. The function of sensitivity is self-explanatory. The body still does not have power. You want to seek out the meaning and cultivate power. It's not easy to recognize this kind of movement. If a student only gets T'ai Chi boxing's form, it will create a strong body and this benefit will last a lifetime.

The second step:

To inherit T'ai Chi boxing's method you must learn the T'ai Chi boxing form and gain sensitivity. To get the real skill of application is very difficult because this step must be sought out. Even though the T'ai Chi boxing method is based on four ounces toppling a thousand pounds, if the student cannot connect properly with the thousand pounds, then he could not even move a hundred pounds.

Students pass through the practice of sensitivity and study balance (T'ai Chi boxing's form). Afterwards they feel a sinking of weight; it is sort of an energy. This is called hip energy and is just the appearance of a strong body and that is all. It is still not enough to respond to an enemy. If you encounter a strong, young, and majestic man, you need to know how to solve his offense. You need to strike him, but what do you make use of? And you don't know. To know this you must seek out T'ai Chi's method.

Research and study the application of techniques; add to your own strength. Today's practice method compared to earlier ones is different. You want to change from soft and slow to hard. This is to comprehend T'ai Chi boxing's meaning of the hard and soft method. It is said: First ask to expand, afterwards ask to contract— do it this way. To arrive at this stage of development in T'ai Chi boxing's style you must forge it, break it open. Practice one style completely. It can be soft and hard, quick or slow. Know how to use the method's changes. Practice T'ai Chi boxing's entire boxing style to completion. Afterwards again and again practice Push hands. Take a beating, accept bitterness. You don't want to waste many years' time.

The T'ai Chi boxing method means you are able to use varied combinations of hard and soft. The third step and the final stage of skill in regard to T'ai Chi boxing's meaning of the hard and soft method is already harmoniously blended on one stove. Then, strength is added. People say that T'ai Chi boxing uses Ch'i and that it really does not use strength. Ch'i is soft practice, and therefore T'ai Chi boxing is not a hard practice. This really is to know one but not the other part of the method. You must know that T'ai Chi boxing's practice of Ch'i is the third step of skill.

So it is said: Practice vitality and change it to Ch'i, practice Ch'i and change it to spirit, practice spirit and return to the void. Vitality is the sum total of a person's mental and physical strength, and this power creates a bank account. What can you depend on to change Ch'i to spirit? To practice Ch'i and cultivate Ch'i are two different things. To practice Ch'i you must first have Ch'i in your bank account, and then you can practice the cultivation of Ch'i. For example: An old, weak, sick man can cultivate Ch'i. The first step is to learn T'ai Chi boxing's form, then you want to cultivate Ch'i and get to the second step of practising Ch'i's bank account. But if you only depend on the soft and slow T'ai Chi form, you are not able to forge the Ch'i, so you must seek the T'ai Chi method to increase your strength.

In the beginning, the Ch'i and strength are not separated and are called Ch'i-Strength. The strength is collected in the muscles and called body strength. The Ch'i is concealed in the blood and called blood Ch'i. Because the Ch'i and strength are not separated, ask yourself whether without Ch'i strength can come out? Ask yourself whether without strength, the Ch'i is enough to use? So, Ch'i without strength is like looking at a patient at the point of death, about to take his final breath. Are you telling me this last breath can attack a formidable enemy? The Ch'i does not leave strength, and the strength does not leave the Ch'i. Having the strength of Ch'i, however, can be used, and then you have enough to carry out the the third step of tapping the Ch'i's bank account. Ch'i and strength are united. It is called making energy. It is T'ai Chi boxing's most indispensable thing.

With regard to the boxing classics it is said: The most soft and afterward the most hard. Students misunderstand its meaning. This is the study of the theory of relativity, so the reverse of softness is hardness. This is the physical part of the theory of relativity and is also a science. To learn this you have to track the footprints of history. So, the Kuang P'ing school is the practice method which combines the hard and soft. It is founded on scientific principles. Most people like to accept the mysterious and usually don't understand the science included in the mystery. There are many students who don't get this because they have not received the real teaching, and so they do their practice without thinking. Boxing classics say: The ultimate softness, then the ultimate hardness. Also it is said: First the T'ai Chi form, the softness of sensitivity, and afterwards the T'ai Chi method. Then harmoniously blend in Shao Lin's hardness. The boxing classics say: First expand then contract. Expanding is boxing's relaxation and T'ai Chi's form. It belongs to the soft. Contracting is the strength gathered in the center. Then with the T'ai Chi method you can encounter the idea of hard. "Can be soft, can be hard." T'ai Chi contains the Yin and Yang, the two Ch'i's. The nature of Yin is soft, the nature of Yang is hard. So, T'ai Chi boxing must have soft and hard combined together. T'ai Chi—Yin Yang. If it is completely soft, then it is not T'ai Chi boxing at all.

The third step:

This is to comprehend T'ai Chi boxing's achievement. It is to receive T'ai Chi boxing's ultimate skill. It is to pass through and enter the boundary of spiritual change. You can say that this skill is T'ai Chi boxing's personality and the boxing art's special characteristic. It is T'ai Chi boxing's most mysterious abode. This achievement is the mysterious ability of changing from fast to slow. The achievement means the study of man's body and the method of internal achievement. It is the interior which cause the changes, rising like waves, and this is called the great chariot. Chariot means success. Its meaning is the same as the Taoist attainment.

The T'ai Chi boxing form is the first step for learning the practice of energy, and then you pass through and comprehend the second step, which is the T'ai Chi method. Then the entire body is filled up and brimming with energy. After this step it is time for the third step. In accordance with the T'ai Chi boxing form, you can make use of and get the skill of combining the fast and slow energy changes. It seems soft as cotton with no strength. In stillness there is movement, and in movement there is stillness. Naturally your Taoist breathing arises, from which comes the sum total of your mental and physical strength, and you brim with energy. Forge and change the Ch'i and mix it into the blood, then the whole body will be understood. This state of mind is what Mr. Pan Hou gave to Wang Ch'iao Yu. It is called without leaving a trace; the whole body passes through space.

The entire body is comfortable when striking. For a second you are relaxed, for a second you are tight. This makes the Ch'i circulate everywhere without impediment. This feeling only comes to a person of comprehension. Eventually, you change the Ch'i to spirit and practice the spirit and return to the void. Then the whole body is full of vitality, Ch'i, and spirit. These three things must be blended. Then the nerve tissue, the muscles, the internal organs, the blood vessels, and the breathing will reach a strength which you can't imagine. It appears soft as cotton with no strength; powerful energy appears as if it is nothing, a shadow, unfathomable. It is T'ai Chi boxing's great achievement of skill. Then the body is like the perfect Buddhist body with no peer.

T'ai Chi boxing's achievement is in action. If students only get T'ai Chi boxing's form, then it is called "small success" but it will provide enough strength to enjoy its benefits for a lifetime. If you can get to T'ai Chi boxing's method, then it is called "medium success" and you will be able to prevail over an enemy and defend yourself. In the event you reach the final stage of the T'ai Chi achievement, then it is called "great success." You have created a perfect body and discovered a mystery which is unimaginable.

In bygone days, the Kuang P'ing school used the hard and soft practice method. It is the Yang family's real teaching. The Pei Ching school had a completely soft training method, and students merely got the form and that was all. When Master Wang Ch'iao Yu was alive he often said with a heavy sigh that when today's people learn T'ai Chi boxing, they only get the T'ai Chi boxing form. Their bodies are like the duckweed, with no foundation on which to stand. They waste words about T'ai Chi's inner achievement. The real masters were not willing to teach the effortless way, and the students generally were not willing to do the bitter practice required, so they move around like a pretty dance and that is all.

T'ai Chi Boxing's Definition and its Motion

C'hang San Feng passed down T'ai Chi boxing. It is T'ai Chi's form, created in accordance with the classic Chinese "Book of Changes" the I Ching, using the ideas of reason, character, and appearance. The original works of Confucius called it the scope of heaven and earth. How do we understand reason, character, and appearance? Appearance is the physical description and is T'ai Chi's form. The character is the spiritual force and is T'ai Chi's method. The reason is profound reasoning and is T'ai Chi's achievement. You first get to know the form, then you awake to T'ai Chi's method, and later to T'ai Chi's achievement. If these three skills are gained from intense study, then you are in possession of complete mastery.

Examine T'ai Chi's circular form. Contained in it are Yin and Yang, the two fish. The outer form is circular in every movement. The Yin and Yang symbol of the two fish represents Yin and Yang, the two Ch'i's. Yin's Ch'i is soft and Yang's Ch'i is hard. This is what the T'ai Chi boxing's hard and soft method originated from in its unpolished form. The T'ai Chi is originally from the Wu Chi. When the universe began, T'ai Chi was born from the Wu Chi and the two ideas began. Separate Yin and Yang and you get the four appearances or four seasons, and they dwell in the five elements. All things rise up and return to their root.

T'ai Chi's profound achievement is to rely upon this reasoning. Skill from nothing is practiced to something. From something it is changed to nothing. The spiritual achievement is an obscure and hidden mystery. The Ch'i along with strength has the appearance of nothing yet it reaches the summit. Enter the spiritual change. Opponents are unable to see the hand go out, and your form is very difficult to understand. This is T'ai Chi boxing's ultimate result. This is the real boxing art's practice method.

The Ancient Poem of the Universal Post

The universal post is a mystical form of martial arts
We can never fully understand the way it is done
It seems like an embrace with a smiling face
You use your strength from within
You are relaxed and use no force
It is like clouds floating in the wind from all directions
You use forces from the universe to substantiate your strength
Your strength comes from your breathing
You do not hold fast, leaving a lot of room to move
You do not bend to greater strength
So smoothly you move and so naturally
Your breathing and your limb movements should not be impeded
It is like moving in space
In and out of the highest peaks and clouds
Gliding through air and clouds
Floating along with the winds
Graceful yet composed
Always contain calmness and peace
Head upheld high with pride
You embrace the world below you
As clear and pure as an underground brook
Like lead turning into silver spinning to the moon
Looking into an antique mirror to look deep into your soul
Your cup is filled to the brim
Absolutely free of restraint and free of self
You could fly as though you had wings
Head towards the limitless horizon

Like throwing a pebble into water
The circles get larger and larger
With your hands you push open the limits of the universe
You embrace from within
Heaven and earth and the ten thousand things capture your thoughts
The eyes look outside with determination
Up and down your strength flows
You push and you embrace continuously
Your thoughts should be pure
This should clear your mind
This should curb all illness
You always return to the center
You can attack or defend at will
You must have a will of iron
The principle of this is to strengthen
To go for happiness and health
Your body will benefit from this
This has been handed down from the ancients
This form of exercise can help you without limits

This poem is related to an exercise that entails no movement. It is practiced as a still posture which is held for one hour a day after the practice of the forms. It is standing meditation and expresses mind over body.

The sixty-four movements of Kuang P'ing T'ai Chi

1. Strike palm to ask Buddha

2. Grasp the bird's tail

3. Single whip

4. White stork cools it's wings

5. Brush Knee and twist step

6. Deflect, parry, and punch

7. Step up apparent close up

8. Carry tiger to mountain

9. Fist under elbow

10. Step back and repulse the monkey

11. Slow palm slanting flying

12. Left and right raise hand

13. Flying pulling up force

14. Fan through the arm

15. Green dragon comes out of the water

16. Turn body step up and grasp the bird's tail

17. Single whip

18. Cloud hand

19. High pat on horse

20. Left and right separation of legs

21. Turn the body and kick with leg

22. Wind blowing lotus leaf

23. Finger block up with fist

24. Turn around kicks, two feet up

25. Step up deflect, parry, and punch

26. Retreat with arms beside body

27. Foot kicks up forward

28. Turn the body and kick

29. Enter step deflect, parry, and punch

30. Step up apparent close up

31. Carry tiger to mountain

32. Chop opponent with fist

33. Diagonal single whip

34. Part the wild horse's mane

35. Diagonal single whip

36. Fair lady works at shuttles

37. Turn the body and grasp the bird's tail

38. Single whip

39. Cloud hands
40. Single whip down
41. Golden cock stands on one leg
42. Repulse the monkey
43. Slow palm slanting flying
44. Left right raise hands
45. Flying pulling up step
46. Fan through the arm
47. Strike ears with both fists
48. Through sky cannon
49. Single whip
50. Cloud hands
51. Single whip
52. High pat on horse
53. Cross wave of water lily
54. Downward fist
55. Step up and grasp the bird's tail
56. Single whip
57. Cloud hands
58. Single whip down
59. Step up to form seven stars
60. Retreat to ride tiger
61. Slant the body, turn the moon
62. Water lily kick
63. Shoot tiger with bow
64. Left right grasp the bird's tail